Your DIVINE PURPOSE

Fulfilling your apostolic assignment
and bringing Heaven to Earth.

Copyright © 2023 by Paul
Manwaring

All rights reserved. No part of this publication may be used or reproduced, stored in a retrieval system or transmitted in any form or by any means without written permission from the publisher, except in the case of brief quotations embodied in critical articles and reviews. For more information, visit paulmanwaring.com.

Scripture quotations, unless otherwise indicated, are taken from the New American Standard Bible, Copyright © 1960, 1962, 1963, 1968, 1971, 1972,
1973, 1975, 1977, 1995 by the Lockman Foundation. Used by permission. All rights reserved. Scripture taken from the New King James Version of the Bible. Copyright © 1982 by Thomas Nelson, Inc. Used by permission. All rights reserved.

Written for Your DIVINE PURPOSE, developed by PaulManwaring.
www.paulmanwaring.com

SPECIAL MARKET SALES
Organisations, church's, pastors and small group leaders can receive special discounts when purchasing this book from PaulManwaring.com. For more information, please send an email to paul@paulmanwaring.com

Foreword

Leading people in a great move of God, in the mystery of faith, or in the midst of trying times is no small feat. Paul Manwaring has been a key player in cultivating and keeping the apostolic culture at Bethel Church through many shifting seasons — he quite simply is a genius. His deep friendship and leadership are a gift to this house. In his latest book The Divine Purpose, he brilliantly explains God's original design for apostleship that is applicable to today. Apostleship can feel like an ancient concept or an archaic framework — many have argued that apostles and prophets are not for today while others have embraced apostleship to control a congregation's hierarchy. But the truth is God created a five-fold ministry to see the Church live in the fullness of what it was created for; for saints to be equipped in the works of service. Yet, we have often tiptoed around the idea and smuggled the significance of the five-fold ministry in the modern-day Church. But I'd propose God never intended for apostles and prophets to exit the scene and vanish from Church leadership, nor for the Body to be built on the shoulders of simply pastors and teachers trying to hold down the roles and responsibilities of leadership.

Yet, the Church has highlighted the importance and significance of pastors, teachers, and evangelists leaving a large population wondering where their purpose and significance lie and what it truly means to "be sent". Paul profoundly states "You are apostolic and you are sent by Jesus—whoever you are, whatever you do for work or "ministry," wherever you go, and whatever church you call home. Jesus did not say that we are only sent "if…", He said we are sent by Him."

Now, let me be clear, I understand the heart longing to know if you have been called to an office or even the simple desire to better understand the God-ordained purpose of a prophet, evangelist, pastor, apostle, and teacher. It can often feel elusive and enigmatic to determine if you have been called to an office yourself. It can be even more confusing if the Church largely preaches and portrays solely pastors, evangelists, and teachers. It is detrimental not only to the Body but to society when we silence the role of apostleship. Mankind's lens often becomes tainted by their fears and failures, causing them to read between the lines and create a philosophy that fits their comfortability and reasoning. Yet, mystery is a key to apostolic culture. When we fear mystery we reject a foundation of our faith because we then limit God to our own understanding. However, we serve a

God with a much greater frame of reference; that has knit divine purpose within the DNA of a diverse ecosystem and function in the Body that is needed to bring Heaven to Earth. If you have wondered how to live out your apostolic assignment, hunger for revival, and desire to see Heaven on earth, Your Divine Purpose will be a catalytic resource on the journey of stepping into the fullness of your divine calling.

Kris Vallotton
Senior Associate Leader, Bethel Church, Redding, CA
Co-Founder of Bethel School of Supernatural Ministry
Author of fifteen books, including The Supernatural Ways of Royalty, Spiritual Intelligence, and Uprising.

Dedication

To all the Christians who have struggled to find their place in church and life. The reformers, revivalists and renaissance men and women who have sometimes compared themselves with those 'paid to go to church' and felt less valuable to the Kingdom of Heaven.

The doctors and carers, the teachers and the civil servants, the engineers and city planners, the explorers, designers, architects and scientists, the social workers and the builders and makers of homes, houses and families.

To the mothers and fathers who stay at home to raise the next generation.

To the ones whose dedication is to making life better for others, the government leaders, police and emergency workers, the entrepreneurs, and creatives.

You are the sent ones. Sent from heaven to earth and through the church sent to expand heavens influence on earth.

You are needed. Graphic designers with moral character, computer scientists who understand ethics, truth and philosophy.

This book is dedicated to you. A field guide for SENT ONES. An apostolic assignment for those who have not felt empowered by an apostle, but sometimes only felt valued for what they do in church. Thank you for bringing change to your world. Making history one family meal at a time.

Don't compare, believe your story, go to church, be the church but do not fret if your call takes you to work outside of the church. For it is heaven on earth we pray for and a whole earth, not just a church filled with his glory.

Only a fully empowered family of believers can achieve this.

We need you.

This is for you.

Paul

Your DIVINE PURPOSE

Fulfilling your apostolic assignment and bringing Heaven to Earth

CONTENTS:

INTRODUCTION	1
SECTION 1: DEFINING THE APOSTOLIC	**7**
1. You Are Apostolic	7
2. Understanding the Fivefold	13
3. The Apostle	19
4. The Apostolic Prophet	25
5. The Apostolic Evangelist	31
6. The Apostolic Pastor	37
7. The Apostolic Teacher	43
8. First Apostles	47
9. Unity: A Goal of the Apostolic	55
10. The Defining Factor	61
SECTION 2: YOUR APOSTOLIC ASSIGNMENT	**65**
11. Times and Seasons	65
12. Revival	71
13. Reformation and Transformation	77
14. Renaissance	83
15. Building on the Foundation of Others	89
16. Overcoming Secularism	95
17. An Apostolic Culture	101
18. Change	109
19. Relational Government	115
20. The Supernatural	121
SECTION 3: APOSTOLIC LEADERSHIP	**127**
21. The Marketplace	127
22. Organization: The Sum of Many Parts	133
23. The Apostolic and the Gift of Government (Administration)	141
24. Structure and Organizational Leadership	147
25. Accountability	153
26. Empowerment and an Apostolic Culture	161
27. Apostolic Families	167
28. Big People	173
29. Success or Succession?	179
30. Maintaining Momentum	185

SECTION 4: EMBRACING AN APOSTOLIC LIFESTYLE   **191**

    31. Perseverance   191
    32. Mystery   197
    33. Justice   203
    34. Excellence   209
    35. Worship   215
    36. Faith and Hope   221
    37. Sonship and Inner Healing   229
    38. Covering   237
    39. Destiny   243
    40. Dreams   249
    41. Discipleship   255
    42. Sent   261

CONCLUSION: AN APOSTOLIC COMMISSION   **268**

Introduction

Earlier this year, one of the spiritual fathers in my life said that he felt I should build something. As I heard him say that, I knew that he was correct. But what should I build?

We talked about a school of leadership or a church plant, and while they both have great attraction, they do not fit my current season.

The words of Jesus recorded in John chapter 20 have long been important to me. "As the Father sent me so I send you" (John 20:21). As I studied the context of this verse, it became clear to me that it had a greater relevance for my ministry and the days in which we live than I previously realized.

In John 20:19-23, the scene opens up on the evening of the first day of the week. In other words, the very first resurrection Sunday. The disciples were locked in a room, for fear of the Jews.

They were afraid because the city was in chaos after a most dramatic weekend.

Their way of life had been dramatically removed from them; they had left their careers and traveled with Jesus for three years. What would they do next?

They felt powerless as they watched the one who raised the dead, die himself. They had been betrayed by one of their closest friends and watched him betray their leader and friend.

It was into this scenario that Jesus appeared. He, as always, had the answer for all four of their questions and fears, even if none of those fears had been articulated.

In four statements, the resurrected Jesus declared the answers to what had not been asked.

Twice He said "Peace be with you." This is a reminder of the peace mandate: there at His birth, continued through His ministry, and now still the answer in a chaotic world.

Next, He gave the mandate of being SENT. The disciples' questions about their loss of purpose and way of life were answered as Jesus commissioned them to continue the work.

Then, He empowered them. Jesus said to the disciples, "Receive the Holy Spirit." Whatever the reason for the timing, it answered their feeling of powerlessness and reminded them of what they had already seen. Paul would later write in Romans 8:11 that the same Spirit who raised Jesus from the dead, dwells in us.

Finally, He instructed them to forgive, teaching them of the power of forgiveness for themselves and those that they forgive. As I studied these verses and this idea of being sent, and sending others, I knew what I wanted to build: a way to continue the movement that Jesus started that first resurrection Sunday.

I wish I could tell you that I heard an audible voice, but I did sense a deep confirmation of a theme in my life. It is not so much about starting a movement, but fueling one that has already begun.

I want every believer to know that they are sent. That, in a sense, we are sent twice. We're sent once as Jesus said, and we're then sent again through the church, into the world, to expand the influence of King Jesus.

This remarkable assignment begins with the First Apostle, Jesus, and is therefore an apostolic assignment. He is the one who is sent and the one who sends. Jesus was sent by the Father, but then He sent us. We are sent by Him; and from Him, all things apostolic flow.

The word apostolic is often hidden, distorted, complicated, and distanced from our understanding of identity and assignment as followers of Jesus. It is my intention to change that.

You are apostolic and you are sent by Jesus— whoever you are, whatever you do for work or "ministry," wherever you go, and whatever church you call home. Jesus did not say that we are only sent "if...", He said we are sent by Him. As we grab hold of this with an internal awareness, it will affect everything we say, do, and believe. I am sure that every one of us desires the experience of being sent on an important and prestigious assignment: to be trusted, believed in, resourced, and sent to do more than we could ever dream of, with the backing of the One who sent us.

This is the opportunity and invitation given to all mankind. All we need to do is accept the apostolic assignment outlined in the words Jesus taught us to pray: "On earth as it is in Heaven." Remarkably, He didn't only teach us to pray the words, but He sent us to co-labour in it, empowered us to do it, and believed we would see it.

In John 1:14, John describes Jesus' assignment as "The Word became flesh," which creates the beautiful picture of Christ as God's letter, sent to us all. One of the most significant pieces of guidance in my life came in the form of a letter. It would not be an exaggeration to say that it entirely set the course of my life.

The following pages are my letters to all believers, the sent ones.

However you use these letters—as a book, a reference, a study guide—the goal is to demystify the overall interpretation of all things apostolic as they relate to the individual sent one and the churches that send us out.

The world feels chaotic, many feel a loss of purpose and are looking for something more. It is easy to feel powerless as we watch and experience the frailty of life on earth. So many are disappointed, feeling betrayed and let down by others. The context of our current season is so similar to that of the disciples' season on that first resurrection Sunday, and the words of Jesus still contain everything we need.

My goal is to help believers see that they carry peace into a chaotic world, can find purpose as they embrace the words of Jesus, have access to all the power that they need, and that their souls can participate in the reconciliation of all humanity.

We are meant to be equipped in family, encountering the presence, and sent as emissaries into the world. As Jesus said, "Just as the Father SENT me, I SEND you" (MSG, emphasis added).

You are our letter, written in our hearts, known and read by all men.

2 Corinthians 3:2

As thou didst send me into the world, I also have sent them into the world.

John 17:18

SECTION 1: DEFINING THE APOSTOLIC

1. You Are Apostolic

In John 17:18, The Apostle John recorded that Jesus said to His father, "As thou didst send me into the world, I also have sent them into the world." In Greek, the word used in this verse for "send" is *apostellō*—the root of the word apostle—which implies setting free, empowering, trusting, or believing in someone.

What comes to mind when you hear the words apostle or apostolic? Does it apply to you? Does it apply only to someone who holds the title of Apostle?

If you doubt that Jesus was talking to you in this verse, I suggest that you read the context: "I am not asking on behalf of these alone, but for everyone who believes on account of their words" (John 17:20).

Many things have developed in our world and churches since John 17:18 was first written. Regardless, this is a clear statement that all of us in relationship with Jesus Christ are sent ones, and therefore our mindset should be apostolic in nature.

There are many discussions and organizations built around the words "apostle" and "apostolic." There are debates over whether the idea of the apostolic ended with "the twelve," and even divisions over the use and application of the title, Apostle.

When considering the five gifts of Christ to the Church listed in Ephesians 4:11 (apostles, prophets, evangelists, pastors, and teachers) I want to suggest that the outcomes of the gifts are more important than the actual titles. We read in Ephesians 4:12 that each of the gifts is given to the Church for the equipping of the saints for the work of ministry. That being the case, it should look like this:

The pastor equips the saints to be pastoral.
The evangelist equips the saints to be evangelistic.
The prophet equips the saints to be prophetic.
The teacher equips the saints to be teachers/teachable.

If the above list is correct, then the Apostle equips the saints to be apostolic. However, when asked, most believers say that they are not apostolic. We've somehow come to believe that the term apostolic describes the Apostle rather than the outcome of being led and influenced by an Apostle.

That misunderstanding is the purpose for this book. An apostolic move of God requires that all believers realize and embrace their designation as sent ones: apostolic members of the body, sent by Jesus.

Perhaps the problem is that you have not found "your" apostle yet, the one who will teach and equip you to be apostolic. But even then, you can find your apostle in the First Apostle. Hebrews 3:1 says that Jesus is the SENT ONE, the first Apostle, and every other apostle after Him should equip the saints to be apostolic.

So if Jesus is your personal savior, you are apostolic. As you are influenced by Him and choose to live like Him, you will learn to walk in the apostolic.

As soon as we recognize that we are all intended to be apostolic, we need to change the way we think—the best translation of repentance that I know.

Repentance is not always about turning away from things that are wrong, but (and perhaps more importantly) thinking and doing what is correct and more glory-filled. Paul said to the Romans that all have sinned and fallen short of the glory. In my experience, when reviewing this verse, we tend to focus on the word sinned, usually in the context of doing wrong things.

The meaning of the original word translated into English as "sinned" is actually better defined as "missing the mark," or falling short of the target. With this in mind, we need to repent not just for falling short of the target in regard to the things we may have done, but we also need to reposition ourselves to live from a higher calling—change the way we think.

Here are a list of prompts to help us all to change the way we think about being apostolic:

It's a mindset that comes from being under the influence of an Apostle.
It started with Jesus (Hebrews 3:1).
Every Kingdom-minded believer is apostolic.
It means you are sent.
The Apostle's job is to equip all the saints to be apostolic.
Its cry is "On earth as it is in Heaven."
It is relational in nature.
It carries and creates Heaven's culture.
It knows no limits ("Greater works than these shall you do").
It pursues, reproduces, and represents Jesus.

This book is an invitation to you, follower of Jesus Christ, to believe that *you* are apostolic. Yes, you! Not only are you apostolic, but understanding the apostolic is a key to understanding how to live out your assignment here on earth.

I know, however, that we have some ground to cover before we all feel comfortable embracing our apostolic identities.

Let's get started.

Review
Which aspect of the apostolic is new you? Are there any aspects that particularly challenge you?

Declare
What will you declare about being apostolic?

Reflect
What does it mean to be SENT from Heaven? Where and to whom are you SENT? Who do you look to as an apostle in your life?

He gave some as Apostles,

and some as Prophets,

and some as evangelists,

and some as pastors and teachers.

Ephesians 4:11

2. Understanding the Fivefold

The fourth chapter of Ephesians contains thirty-two verses, and yet it feels that we pay unbalanced attention to verse eleven. That one verse causes many to ask me, and I am sure many other leaders, for our view of the fivefold.

Ephesians 4:11 is the only verse in the Bible that lists the fivefold all together: Apostle, Prophet, Evangelist, Pastor, and Teacher. And yet it attracts so many questions!

Are there just five gifts of Christ?

Are there more, and if there are, what are they?

What does it mean for us as we lead the church two thousand years later?

Should every church have all five of the fivefold on the leadership team?

There is much to be gained from studying Ephesians 4:11, which clearly contains great guidance. However, some readers reach conclusions about the entire structure of the church from this one verse. It is, I conclude, dangerous to be too rigid in our understanding, interpretation, and application of Ephesians 4:11. It has been said that, while it is foolish to worship angels, it is also foolish to ignore them. I suggest that it is foolish to base all of our "churchmanship" off of one verse, but it is equally foolish to ignore that verse.

The passage in Ephesians 4 is vital for the Church and a healthy application of the five gifts is essential. Yet, we shouldn't use it to build a church with five offices. That endeavor is potentially as distracting as ignoring the apostolic and prophetic in our ministries. We must ensure that, in our desire to embrace all of these five gifts, we don't overlook the purpose and outcome of this portion of scripture and the context in which the five gifts are listed.

The focus of this book is the apostolic and the apostolic is a mindset: a set of beliefs and behaviors that become a lens through which we can live and view other aspects of the Christian life, as well as the advancement of the Kingdom of Heaven on earth. Ephesian 4:11 gives us one such lens.

I have fallen in love with this chapter of Ephesians as a gift that keeps on giving. The context in which we find the fivefold verse is extraordinary:

Verses 1-3:   The unity of the Spirit.
> *Verses 4-6: The singleness of the body, Spirit, hope, Lord, faith, and baptism.*
> *Verses 7-11: The gifts of Christ.*
> *Verse 12: The purpose of equipping the saints.*
> *Verse 13: The resulting unity of faith, knowledge of the Son of God, maturity of believers.*

Verse 14: The outcome: we are no longer tossed around, tricked, or deceived.
Verse 15: Growing up to be like Jesus, the head.
Verse 16: The whole body working efficiently and in the excellence of love.

Not to mention the remaining sixteen verses of this rich chapter.

We need the fivefold because we need the outcomes the fivefold should bring. A fivefold approach that does not expect to see unity, maturity, Christlikeness, a lack of deceived believers, and a body built up in love is greatly missing the mark. The purpose of the fivefold is to equip the saints. In whatever capacity you lead, the challenge is the same for all of us: How are we being equipped, and what fruit are we expecting to see?

Ephesians 4:11 is leading us to embrace these gifts, see through the eyes of Heaven's ministers, and be equipped accordingly. The prophetic lens brings tomorrow into today and values the unseen world. The evangelist's lens is all about the good news of Jesus and the needs of mankind. Teachers carry a lens of the word and the Spirit, and pastors approach life through the lens of caring for each other. And the apostolic lens is that of being sent to bring change.

Each does so for the purpose of a body walking in unity and love.

Review
What has your view of the fivefold been? Think of a time when you have sat under/ learned from someone who held a fivefold office. What was the fruit of that time?

Declare
What can you declare about the fivefold that will help shift your perspective?

Reflect
Reflect on how God has used the fivefold to shape your walk with Him and equip you for what you are doing today. What can you find to be thankful for?

Paul, an apostle (not sent from men nor through the agency of man, but through Jesus Christ, and God the Father, Who raised Him from the dead).

Galatians 1:1

3. The Apostle

What is an Apostle? Many books have been written on this topic. It is often used as a title for many leaders, and yet I suspect that many believers are either confused or in some way misled regarding its meaning. Some church cultures call all their leaders pastors, and others give some the title of apostle. In both cases, this can fail to reflect the true gift of the title holder. In many instances, apostle is merely a title given to the leader according to the culture of that organization.

In a book on the apostolic, it would be remiss of me not to write a description of the Apostle. I will follow this with the other four gifts listed in Ephesians 4:11, often called office holders.

Jesus is the first Apostle (Hebrews 3:1). That's a good place to start. He was the first "sent one" and the first sender of others; the model of the supernatural being fully available; the embodiment of prophet, teacher, evangelist, and pastor serving the Father's will on earth. He was the one who taught us to pray perhaps the greatest commission of them all, "On earth as it is in Heaven."

In other words, Jesus the Apostle was the Eternal Father and Eternal Son, the first disciple of men with the goal of bringing Heaven to earth.

It is easy to resort to calling someone an apostle because of what they have built, and in some cases there is nothing wrong with that. Networks are formed, church planting multiplied, and great influence achieved, and the title rightly reflects the great value of that ministry. But these must not be the only reasons for calling someone an apostle, or for someone to assume the title.

What is striking to me is that when we look at the example of Jesus and Paul as apostles, we don't immediately focus on what they built, but rather on who they were, what happened when they showed up, and how they influenced those around them. Both were sent: Jesus by the Father from Heaven (John 17:18) and Paul by Jesus (Acts 9:15-16).

Using that as a starting point, my approach to understanding what defines an apostle is a list of five dynamics. These five things are, in my opinion, essential, although they are not necessarily the complete picture.

1. **Commissioned**: Being sent must be the first dynamic. Sent from somewhere and someone to achieve change, transformation, restoration, increase, and redemption for the King and His Kingdom.

If I use the illustration of the Romans when they occupied other lands, which is the likely origin of the word apostle, we can see that the apostle was sent from Rome to influence that place to become more like Rome. The Roman Apostle was sent from Rome with a specific assignment.

2. **Heaven to Earth:** The Apostle must live his or her life from Heaven's perspective, believing in the supernatural and raising a generation that minister the works of Jesus. Whatever achievements are added to that are of lesser priority, although in the case of an Apostle, everything else will be affected by this priority and they will cause everyone to be influenced by it. Just as the Roman apostle lived with Rome in mind, so Christ's Apostles must live with Heaven and its potential in mind.

3. **Whole Body Leadership:** I believe that the most qualified Apostles are those who have, through their life and ministry, demonstrated the other four gifts. This equips them to draw the whole body together and for each to find their place. The Apostle draws people together and has the ability to see through others' eyes with the perspective of Heaven.

4. **Relational Context:** The language of the Apostle is family. "God so loved…that He gave His only Son" (John 3:16). "As the Father has sent me, so I send you" (John 17:18). There must be a relational context to the Apostle and the Apostle's ministry. They must be followed as an Apostle, have peers who are also Apostles, and have fathers and mothers who believe in their gift and assignment as an Apostle. These are essential elements of the relational model.

They must also know that they are adopted sons and lead from that place in humility, as one sent to serve. We see this so clearly in Paul's description of Jesus in Philippians 2, and in Jesus' own words: He came to serve, not to be served. Paul sums this up in his description of Apostles being the foundation, serving upwards, rather than through a top-down hierarchical model (Ephesians 2:20).

5. **An Apostolic Culture:** The effect of the Apostle on the people around them is that the people become apostolic. Jesus chose twelve men and discipled them, and they transitioned to being Apostles. Do we train people to be Apostles? This is a part of the process, but my inclination is that we create an apostolic culture in which we disciple people and watch Apostles emerge. The fruit of this process is maturity among believers, who live as apostolic companies or families of people led by prophets, pastors, evangelists, teachers, and in this case, apostles.

Review
Read Paul's story in Acts 9:1-22 and Acts 13:1-12. What features of the Apostle can you see in Paul's journey?

Declare
What will you declare to reinforce what you have learned today?

Reflect
How have you defined an apostle? How would you describe the characteristics and fruit of an apostolic culture?

All are not prophets, are they?

1 Corinthians 12:29

4. The Apostolic Prophet

Of the five gifts listed in Ephesians 4:11, two are selected as foundations of the church. Ephesians 2:20 clarifies that, "Apostles and the Prophets are the foundation of the church." This I believe speaks primarily of the effect of their gifts throughout the whole of the Christian faith and upon the lives of its members. It is clear, though, that there are to be those whose status, title, or office is that of an apostle or prophet, and their assignment is to create apostolic and prophetic people and cultures.

Comparing apostles and prophets, one simple distinction between them, which also connects them, is that the apostle visits Heaven and the prophet visits the future. Of course, it is not as simple as that, but this picture reveals that both must operate in the unseen realm. Neither can function without the indwelling of the Holy Spirit empowering, enabling, gifting, and emboldening them. In this regard, they are distinct from the evangelist, pastor, and teacher who can, in many respects, perform a version of their role without paying heed to the supernatural. That is, however, a limitation that was not intended and has had a major effect on the nature of the Church.

The apostle and prophet portrayed in Ephesians are a partnership. The apostle needs the prophet and vice versa, and the Church needs both. Whether they are both in the same organizational structure is perhaps less important than that they are in each other's lives, and the lives of the Church and the pastor, evangelist, and teacher.

I love the prophetic ministry. My life has been guided by the prophetic for the past twenty years. Especially in the last six, prophecy has been one of the mainstays of our personal decisions and direction in life. Having said that, without a prophetic culture, a prophetic word can very easily be likened to the parable of the sower and the seed. If the soil on which the word falls is solid, rocky, or filled with weeds, then the word will not take root and grow but will quickly shrivel up or be choked or meet too many rocky obstacles.

This is why culture is essential to the ministry of the prophet. Farmers prepare soil; ploughing, fertilizing, and making it ready for growth. The prophet helps to prepare the soil, which is the culture. As the prophet edifies, comforts, and exhorts, the ensuing culture helps prophetic words to take root and grow.

I was given a prophetic word about preaching in stadiums when I had never preached in stadiums before. It would have been easy to dismiss, but the culture around me is one that grabs the prophetic, however impossible it seems. I was sent to Reinhard Bonnke's School of Evangelism less than three months after that word, an indication of the practical behavior that followed our culture and deeply held belief in the power of prophetic words.

I do not believe that you can separate a prophetic culture from an apostolic culture; nor do I think we should even try.

When creating an apostolic culture, I suggest four starter cultures that I call Game Changers: *Hope*, the *Goodness of God*, the *Presence of God*, and *Healing*. They also certainly fit the needs of the prophetic. All four help to create an environment in which a prophetic word can land and take root. Alongside these, *Honor* and *Calling out the Greatness in Each Other* are equally important cultures. Without them, a community is less likely to give, receive, encourage, or activate prophetic words by faith.

The goal of a prophetic (and apostolic) culture is to prophecy from the heart of a good God into hearts of people who know that they are valued by Heaven. This is done in an environment or community where the prophetic words are encouraged, and the people are comforted and built up to live out their prophetic destiny.

Creating a prophetic culture is not dependent on having a prophet on your leadership team, but rather having a prophet in the life of the leader and church. Prophets will equip their people to be prophetic and they will also help to establish a prophetic culture. Prophetic words without a prophetic culture will result in many words not growing to their full potential. The prophetic culture is also essential to the expression of our faith outside of the church—bringing hope, encouragement, and comfort to a troubled world.

A prophetic word is an encounter with the God who knows your future. This truth is central to the role of the apostolic prophet. Together with the apostle, who is pulling Heaven's culture, behavior, and power to earth, the prophet is pulling tomorrow into today.

I expect to see the prophet and the apostle working together. As we embrace the apostle we must expect the prophet alongside. Although I believe that the apostle has a primary effect, I also cannot construct an apostolic family or community in my thinking without the prophet alongside.

Review
Read 1 Corinthians 14:1-12. How does Paul describe the prophetic strengthening the Church? Have you seen any examples of an apostle and a prophet working together? What strikes you about this relationship?

Declare
What can you declare to reinforce the prophetic in your life?

Reflect
Reflect on the prophetic words you have been given. Which would be more easily established within a prophetic culture? What does God want to tell you about these words?

Do the work of an evangelist, fulfill your ministry.

2 Timothy 4:5

5. The Apostolic Evangelist

Evangelists have operated as sent ones perhaps more than any other of the fivefold. That would seem to be a good thing, and in many cases it is: they are the most obvious outreach arm of the Church, sent to carry the good news.

Often, however, they haven't experienced being sent by the Church itself. There is a pressure on them to get cleaned up, to take care of their stuff, and to sort out their theology before the Church is willing to risk their reputation on the newly converted potential evangelist. While this is understandable, it feels like a constraint on their urgency and burning passion to share the good news. The result is that some go out into the world without the support of family. Instead of waiting, having their theology "sorted," and feeling like a square peg in a round hole, they pursue a more independent lifestyle and ministry.

Coupled with this, many of the most passionate converts come to Christ from a place of brokenness, and they need healing so they don't reproduce their dysfunction in their disciples. They also are often very driven individuals. Healing will help them to lead and evangelize from a place of rest rather than drive. The challenge is for this healing to take place in a way that doesn't remove them from their immediate harvest field. It is a delicate balance.

The raw, passionate, radically saved convert is a potential evangelist, a gift of Christ—the Great Evangelist—to the Church. They belong at the government table, equipping the saints for the work of ministry. Their raw passion is often what the Church needs, injecting the desire to reach the lost into every aspect of a church's activities.

We need our evangelists and we need them to stay connected to the world from which they came; it will surely be their first harvest field. But we also need them to be positioned in family and to receive the help they need to be the best that they can be.

They are, in my experience, very often a unique breed, and one which I have come to love and value the more I get to know them. One temptation is to view evangelists as radically saved. Many of them have dramatic stories, for sure, but the truth is that all of us who know, love, serve, and believe in Jesus as Lord and Savior have a radical salvation. We are saved from eternal separation from God and that is radical, although we may not all have such dramatic stories to show for it.

We need to ensure that our understanding of radical salvation does not create or widen a gap between the evangelist and the Church. Instead, we must draw closer together so that we can all partake in different ways in the evangelistic assignment of the Church. To believe that I must have a dramatic story will increase the gap, but to share in a radical salvation will qualify us all.

It is, I believe, the day of the evangelist. There is a desire and a calling of them back to the Church—back to leadership in the Church, equipping the saints, and creating a culture of salvation. They are not to be the ones who do all of the work, but rather the ones who inspire and equip all of us to find our harvest field and serve in it.

The evangelist in an apostolic culture will be valued. They are one of the keys to the growth the apostle desires. By feeling valued, they will also feel at home. I always view the returning prodigal in Luke 15 as a returning evangelist, because I have never met someone saved in such circumstances that did not want to tell others. Like the boy in the story, evangelists need to be valued, given the robe of worth, the ring of trust, the sandal of sonship, and the celebration party. From that place of home—the apostolic family—they will be sent. There will be no need to leave without the backing of a family who believes in them, waits for their return, and shares in the spoils of their adventure. They will not merely be sent, but will also be equippers and senders of everyone, sending them into their unique places of influence and calling.

The apostolic evangelist will have a big picture. They will embrace the Church and the Kingdom: winning souls and discipling while experiencing and contributing to home and belonging. They will, in line with the nature of the apostolic, know that first they are sent. The goal is not to gather first but to be sent into all of the world. They will bring the saved home to a family where they can be loved, healed, discipled, and, in turn, sent out. And they will of course be apostolic first, not merely persuaders of people to receive Christ, but demonstrators of His power.

We need evangelists. Not to build large churches, though that may happen, but to expand the influence of the King and His Kingdom everywhere that they and the saints they serve are sent.

Review
Read the story of the Prodigal Son again in Luke 15, with the lens of the returning evangelist. What stands out to you? Have you been tempted to view some evangelists as radical because their testimony of salvation is radical? What can you do to think differently and narrow that gap?

Declare
List those you describe as evangelists in your own church or ministry. What can you declare over them to help them feel loved and accepted as part of your local church family?

Reflect
Reflect on your own story of salvation. What did God save you from?

And when the Chief Shepherd appears.

1 Peter 5:4

6. The Apostolic Pastor

The words of 1 Peter 5:4 include one of my favorite titles for Jesus. He is the Chief, the first above all shepherds. He is the fulfillment of the prophecy of shepherds in Ezekiel 34. What I love about this prophecy is that the shepherd is expected to:

Strengthen
Heal
Bind Up
Bring Back

Not only that, but the lack of a shepherd is the reason the sheep scatter.

There is a strength to this role, which can easily get lost when we place a pastor in a traditionally gentle personality profile. Instead, the prophecy of shepherds paints the picture of the shepherd who risks the rough terrain to find the lost sheep, who fights the bear and the lion, who pursues, encourages, strengthens, and heals.

The title of pastor is used to describe the leader of the local church in much of the world. In many cases this usage is correct, but unless the pastor has been exposed to the apostolic, the title often limits the organization and the people in it.

We definitely need pastors, but if the pastor determines the culture of the church based on their gift alone, there will almost certainly be huge elements of the apostolic missing from the culture. As with all of the five gifts listed in Ephesians, the pastor needs the apostolic and the apostolic needs the pastoral. All five gift holders need each other. Each one of them contributes uniquely to the culture and the assignment of the body of Christ. As I have noted previously, to be apostolic is a mindset derived from coming under the influence of an apostle. Jesus is the first apostle, but also the Chief Shepherd.

It is possible to pastor without accessing the unseen or the supernatural. This is a temptation, because at times it seems easier and avoids risk. Avoiding the supernatural is often driven by a fear of raising false hope in those we are ministering to. I would suggest, however, that the real problem is not in "false" hope, but in not hoping at all.

The pastor in an apostolic culture must learn to steward the divine tension of pulling Heaven to earth, while living in the reality of not always seeing the answer they believe or pray for. Pastors have a high degree of sensitivity for people: they care, feel pain, desire to fix, and often don't enjoy taking risks.

In Ezekiel 34:1-4, the shepherd is rebuked for not healing the sick. That sounds supernatural to me. You may have heard a lot about false prophets, but it seems from Ezekiel that a "false" pastor will (amongst other things) be one that fails to heal.

The pastoral role can no longer be disconnected from the supernatural, and therefore the apostolic.

The apostolic pastor will embrace:

Pastoring while people wait (keeping hope alive)

Pastoring while they receive (walking by faith)

Pastoring until fully well (celebrating what God is doing)

Pastoring in plenty and in lack (maintaining a culture of abundance)

Pastoring after breakthrough and disappointment (living un-offended)

If the pastor is the Senior Leader of a local church, they, like all of us, need to have the influence of an apostle in their life. After all, Jesus is the Chief Shepherd: the apostolic shepherd.

Review
Choose one of the five things that apostolic pastors need to embrace from the list above. Where do you find this principle in the Bible in the lives of the early church?

Declare
What can you declare to change the way you think about the need for apostolic pastors?

Reflect
What senior leaders can you think of from your own life that are called pastors, and truly have a pastoral gifting? What do you notice about them that inspires or encourages you?

Rabbi, we know that you have come from God as a teacher; for no one can do these signs that You do unless God is with him.

John 3:2

7. The Apostolic Teacher

Of the fivefold gifts, the teacher is the most difficult to define. We often end up calling the theologian among us the teacher. That's a great start, but the reality is that unbelievers also study the Bible and theology; but study and knowledge doesn't change their lives, nor the lives of those they teach.

What sets an apostolic teacher apart is that they are influenced by the supernatural, the unseen, and the Holy Spirit. Studying the book without a relationship will result in tearing the characters and content apart, whereas studying the book with a relationship with the Father, Son, and Holy Spirit will result in the building up of the church and the people who it is made up of.

When Nicodemus addressed Jesus, he recognized that Christ was a teacher sent by God because of the signs confirming that God was with Him. This is helpful for me when defining the teacher—it firmly links fruit to knowledge.

I like to draw a parallel from the definitions of science and technology. Science discovers cause and effect, while technology harvests it for the benefit of mankind. Now let me translate this for teachers. Theology discovers cause and effect and apostolic thinking harvests it for the benefit of mankind. If, therefore, my theology is truly the study of God, then when I practice my theology, it should reveal God the Father. If it doesn't reveal the Father, then I may need to revisit my theology.

When the apostolic teacher teaches, they reveal the Father, and in so doing, help the student to also reveal the Father, become more Christlike, and be filled by the Holy Spirit. So what is the role of the teacher in an apostolic culture? I like to think of them as the stewards, or the banks of the river. They keep a watchful eye on truth in relationship with the Spirit of truth. At the same time, they equip the saints to study God for themselves. They help the Church apply what they learn to the assignment they are given as sent ones, expanding the influence of King Jesus on the earth.

Like the pastor, the teacher may be tempted to stay in the realm of the explainable. The teacher, by nature, wants answers and explanations, but the way of the Kingdom is often unexplainable and mysterious.

The apostolic teacher studies and understands the Word, but never limits what they teach to what can be seen and proven in the natural. Above all, the teacher will help us all to be lifelong learners. The apostolic teacher cannot be an academic alone, they must be a practitioner. Their gift encourages; never discourages. It will not limit, but rather point to the limitless One. At the same time, they will provide anchors, be stewards of principles, and explorers of the unfathomable depths of God.

Review
How do you see those with a gift of teaching in your church? Do you recognize the fruit of the apostolic through their teaching?

Declare
What can you declare about what you have learned in this chapter?

Reflect
Think back to a great teacher you had who inspired you in your walk with God. What was it about them that made them so effective or inspiring?

And God has appointed in the church, first apostles, second prophets, third teachers, then miracles, then gifts of healings, helps, administrations, various kinds of tongues.

1 Corinthians 12:28

8. First Apostles

Upon reading 1 Corinthians 12:28, it can appear to be a statement about hierarchy. "And God has appointed in the church, first apostles...." Sadly, I am sure that it has been interpreted and applied in that way. We could probably discuss the effect of that, but I would rather focus on what the benefits are of putting the apostle first in terms of the influence, perspective, and assignment that they bring.

As I read 1 Corinthians 12:28, especially in conjunction with the order of Ephesians 4:11, I prefer to see the order of gifts as a statement of the primary influence of the fivefold, and therefore of all believers.

Rather than describing a hierarchy, Paul is describing how the perspective, principles, and purpose of the apostle must be first. When something is first, it becomes a foundation upon which everything else is built. That principle was given to us in the prayer Jesus taught us to pray, "On earth as it is in Heaven." That is an apostolic principle: let what is in Heaven be sent to earth.

The Apostle Paul gives us the lens we must see through—the lens of the sent ones. After all, we are seated in Heavenly places. We should see from Heaven's perspective—a perspective which Paul links to the prophetic in declaring the apostle and the prophet are the foundation of the church.

Foundations are first things when building. I love the principles of first things, especially summed up by C.S. Lewis in a 1951 letter to Dom Bede Griffiths: "Put first things first and we get second things thrown in: put second things first & we lose both first and second things." In other words, if we put second things first, we get neither the first nor the second things. But if we put first things first, then we will get both. I suspect that C.S. Lewis was influenced by Jesus's own words, "Seek first the kingdom and all these things will be added unto you" (Matthew 6:33).

By putting the apostolic first, "all these things" that Jesus spoke of will be added. I like to sum it up by saying that seeing His Kingdom is the *goal*, and the apostolic is the *how*.

"Apostles first" is another way of saying that every other gift, not just the fivefold, must carry the apostolic DNA. That DNA was established by Jesus with the twelve disciples. He called them disciples and apostles. They were apostles before He was crucified, resurrected, or left us the Holy Spirit! Jesus called them and modeled His way to them, all with the intention of sending them, because He himself was sent.

The pastor must be an apostolic pastor as must the teacher, prophet, and evangelist—they must all have the same relationship to the apostolic. So too must every follower of Jesus be equipped to know that they are apostolic first, which is the task of the Apostle.

The first lens through which we view things determines what we see, the values we apply, and therefore how we behave. To be apostolic first means that we see through Heaven's eyes, we are aligned with the great assignment of Heaven on earth, we know who and whose we are, and we know that we are sent, resourced, and empowered. When that awareness is placed before everything else, it adds to the expression, beliefs, and behavior of every believer.

I am not at all concerned that Paul was creating a hierarchy in his letter to the Corinthians. Throughout the New Testament, Paul postured himself with humility and considered himself the least. When we read his letters in chronological order, we clearly see his progressive journey of greater humility. We also read other passages that express the apostles and prophets as being the foundation of the Church. This is a beautiful picture showing us that it is on their principles and expressions that all else fits into place and is established. Humility and foundations do not lend themselves to hierarchy, they lend themselves to laying down personal agendas in order to serve the whole.

As I've reflected on the definition of apostle, I've looked at the characteristics of the apostolic, not emphasizing particular activities—such as church planting, or networks, or any men and women who are considered to be apostles—but rather, expressions and outcomes that are biblically and universally connected to apostles.

Below I've listed some of the main ones. There are more, and, of course, each of these can be further dissected and defined. This list simply gives us a starting point.

The apostolic is:

> *An empowering culture that sends, promotes, and celebrates*
> *A shared experience of hope and joy*
> *An emphasis on relationship rather than structure*
> *The demonstration of supernatural power*
> *An assignment to represent Christ, who, in turn, reveals the Father*
> *Strengthening, encouraging, and prophetic interactions with each other*
> *Awareness and value for the unseen realm*
> *An ongoing relationship with God, who speaks today*
> *Instinctively confronting the impossible in faith*
> *Embracing mystery*
> *Building on the foundation of others*
> *Ongoing encounters with God*
> *Perseverance that never quits*

In our quest for the apostolic, these characteristics become attainable for us all.

The principle of our faith is that it starts in our minds. Changing the way we think is the beginning of faith. "First apostles" is just that for me: changing the way I think. Many of us have, perhaps, been exposed to abuses of the apostolic. Maybe the title of Apostle was assumed without the full expression, people self-appointed, and so on. This doesn't mean we abandon the apostolic, but it may require redefinition in our thinking.

I encourage you to put the apostolic first. This is not about a person with a title, it is about taking the words of Jesus to heart: we are all the sent ones, sent with Heaven's perspective, which will affect everything we do. There are Apostles, but I urge you, don't wait until you find one that meets your needs or expectations. Embrace the apostolic assignment of Jesus, and see the world through the lens of being sent.

Review
What are the benefits of the Church being built upon the apostles and prophets? What do you think this looks like in practice? How do you see the revelation of apostleship impacting your life?

Declare
What will you declare to reinforce what you have learned?

Reflect
Reflect on your experience of apostleship. Have you seen it misused? What does God want to redeem for you about it?

That they may be one, just as we are one.

John 17:22

9. Unity: A Goal of the Apostolic

This prayer in John 17 is one of the last recorded prayers of Jesus, the first apostle. It is a prayer for unity, modeled on the unity of God the Father and God the Son.

I have taught often on the shift from denominations first, to apostleships first, a concept that the Church is gradually embracing. This is not a statement against denominations, but rather denominationalism. The most important element of this shift is the use of the word first—once again referencing C.S. Lewis's wisdom, that if we put second things first we get neither the first nor the second.

Some apostleships veer into denominationalism if they focus more on gathering others to their organization. The key elements of the apostolic, however, fully embrace the pursuit of unity even when they have clear doctrinal statements for their denomination. We find identity within our ranks which is often articulated through our doctrinal statements. But this must never be at the exclusion of walking together with the diversity found in the bride of Christ.

We must put the first things first.

> *And the glory which thou hast given Me, I have given to them; that they may be one, just as We are one.*
>
> *John 17:22*

What was the glory which the Father gave the Son? We could discuss this at great length, but one interpretation I suggest is that it is relationship. Jesus received the glory from His Father and gave it to us, and the expected outcome was unity.

The glory which the Father gave the Son as He commissioned (apostled) Jesus comes from the unity of the triune, Heavenly family, and must therefore produce unity when it is applied to the family of believers on earth.

That family on earth is referenced at the start of what most people have called The Lord's Prayer. Jesus teaches us to pray and uses the opening phrase, "Our Father...." Whatever we choose to call this prayer, we see that it begins by drawing us together with our Father. We see this connection reiterated by Paul in Ephesians 3:15: "From whom every family on earth derives its name."

Family, unity, and glory are all interconnected.

In the context of Ephesians Chapter 4, we read:

Being diligent to preserve the unity of the Spirit in the bond of peace. There is one body and one Spirit, just as also you were called in one hope of your calling; one Lord, one faith, one baptism, one God and Father of all who is over all and through all and in all.

Ephesians 4:3-6

I doubt that any of us could write a clearer mandate for a united Bride of Christ. Our challenge is to walk it out.

The apostolic culture is also part of the first things. Putting culture first—rather than doctrine—encourages unity. In other words, if unity depends on agreement, then it always has the potential to divide. Instead, creating a culture in which everyone can participate in the pursuit of Christlikeness encourages unity, without requiring complete agreement.

As we pursue the apostolic, it draws us closer to the unity found in common purpose, common relationship with the Father, and a common mission. Perhaps most powerful is finding a sense of shared purpose, as the closer we get to the front lines of battle, the less our differences will matter. This is not always straightforward and the complexity of issues in our world today—with interwoven political and religious elements—makes even this statement a cause of challenge and disunity as we attempt to walk it out.

What I do know, however, is that being distracted by secondary issues is typically one of the major sources of disunity, whereas finding a primary issue draws us together. Jesus' prayer for unity connects us not just to unity, but to the Father, to a common relationship, to a common mission, to making the relationship of the Father and Son known, and to a common purpose!

Review
Read Ephesians 4:3-6. What strikes you as you read? What does God want to tell you about it?

Declare
What can you declare that reflects your understanding of the connection between unity and the apostolic?

Reflect
How would you have defined unity prior to this discussion? How would you define it now? How can you partner with the glory Jesus gave us to create unity in your sphere of influence?

Truly the signs of an apostle were accomplished among you with all perseverance, in signs and wonders and mighty deeds.

2 Corinthians 12:12

10. The Defining Factor

Of all that I have read, 2 Corinthians 12:12 stands alone in defining the apostle and, therefore, the apostolic. If Heaven is to touch earth, it will be evidenced by demonstrations of power. Carrying the power of Heaven into earth's circumstances will be what defines the apostle and marks the apostolic believer.

This verse helps us understand why Jesus and Paul, in particular, are not identified as apostles because of what they built, but rather they are identified as apostles by what happened when they showed up. Perseverance, signs and wonders, and miracles or mighty works: this is surely the defining factor.

We need apostolic government leaders, business women, teachers, mechanics; we need workers in every sphere of influence who are apostolic. It will, however, require perseverance. Perseverance is the birthplace of hope, and faith is its evidence (Hebrews 12:1). Faith requires that we access the power of the unseen world to bring change to the seen world. It is the nature of the apostolic.

This is a dynamic which requires that we remain rooted in an unseen world from which we have been sent. When we fail to see this and are only influenced by what we can see, we will separate ourselves from the source of power and will miss our apostolic, Heaven-sent assignment.

An apostolic assignment marked by signs, wonders, miracles is for everyone. As I process these thoughts I know that the temptation is to dismiss the idea that a power-based assignment is for all believers, but that is the repeated mistake.

It is why the Church must take its place as one of encounters with the person, power, presence, and principles of Jesus. It is that shared experience that makes us family, and that experience from which we are trained, equipped, and sent out to bring change to our world with supernatural power.

Review
Read 2 Corinthians 12:12. What would it look like to walk in signs, wonders, and mighty deeds in your current sphere of influence?

Declare
What can you declare today to reinforce your belief that you are meant to carry the power of Heaven into earth's circumstances?

Reflect
The author states that an apostolic assignment marked by signs and wonders is for everyone. Does this ring true for you or does it challenge you? What does God want to tell you about your assignment?

Who knows whether you have not attained royalty for such a time as this.

Esther 4:14

SECTION 2: YOUR APOSTOLIC ASSIGNMENT

11. Times and Seasons

What time is it? This is a question (and book/message title) that I have used for some years. Wise men in the Bible were known for having insight into the times and seasons. Knowing what time it is and what we should do as a result is something we need today more than ever. An apostolic move of God is illustrated by people who know the times and seasons from Heaven's perspective.

This idea comes from 1 Chronicles 12:32, which describes the sons of Issachar: they understood the times and knew what to do in them. Here we see a link between their gift and their identity—they had knowledge of who they were and the legacy of their family line tracing back to Jacob. As we see the importance of identity in knowing the times and seasons, it helps us understand the importance of partnering the current apostolic move of God with an inner healing move of God.

Most of us are familiar with Esther 4:14, where Esther is asked, "Who knows if you have not attained royalty for such a time as this." We are a generation who are realizing our identities as sons and daughters of the King, which makes us royalty. This link between identity and the wisdom to know the times and seasons is vital for us today.

I ask again, what time is it? Let me list some elements of the time which I believe we are living in.

Revival Time. The rapid increase in the earth's population and the migration to cities gives us the opportunity to reach millions of people. The fact that the next billion people will be born in the next twelve to fifteen years also tells us that there is a great opportunity for reaching the young. There will be over a billion people under fifteen years of age, which is why a billion soul youth revival is actually possible for the first time in history.

Reformation Time. We live in days of extraordinary change. In fact, change is now something that is more desired than it may ever have been. Our job description as Christians is to bring change. After all, our lives were changed at conversion. We are called to repent, change the way we think, and to make earth like Heaven. Our opportunity in this rapidly changing world is to bring change according to the original created order and the principles birthed at creation.

Renaissance Time. We have extraordinary access to creativity, and it is more easily available than other generations. What will we do with it? The renaissance of the fourteenth to seventeenth centuries offered us a model of creativity and inventiveness, but, sadly, it ended in secular humanism. It is time for a new expression, one which brings glory to God and serves mankind.

These three elements of our time and season converge with who we are as a generation of believers. I believe there are five facets of our generation that enable us to embrace the time and season.

An identity generation. This current generation is focused on our identity as sons and daughters. This is a vital component to stepping into the opportunities of revival, reformation, and renaissance.

A destiny generation. There is a great hunger for purpose and a desire to use our time to make a difference. Knowing who we are leads to asking what we are alive for, where we are going, and what the impact of our lives will be.

A Heaven on earth generation. We now see that millions of Western believers living in cultures with a more scientific worldview are pursuing the supernatural in their lives. We are seeing miracles and healing in places we may never have thought possible.

A Kingdom generation. The teaching of seven mountains (or as I prefer, spheres of influence) is changing how Christians see their daily work. When using the word Kingdom, I am referencing the shift in emphasis from church first to Kingdom first. It is one of the shifts which I see as fundamental, and it is a shift which involves everyone. I would suggest that all believers are twice sent. Sent once from Heaven and sent again through the apostolic family (sending church) to expand the influence of King Jesus everywhere they go and no matter what they do.

A presence generation. This generation carries a desire to not just sing songs, but worship and experience the presence of God. In the presence, we see God's value for us more clearly. Moses worshiped and experienced God, and in that atmosphere received instructions for how to build a house for God using the skill of man's hands. As we worship Him and experience Him, just as Moses did, we can do the same.

If we add up these facets of our generation, and the signs of our time, we see a convergence. We see a world offering incredible opportunity, a Church positioning to send people out, people discovering who they are, and the resources of Heaven increasingly being accessed on earth.

Jesus himself rebuked the disciples for understanding the natural signs but failing to recognize the spiritual signs. In other words, He was exhorting them and us to see time from Heaven's perspective, the view for the sent ones.

We were born for such a time as this.

Review
Read the story of Esther. How do you see her knowledge of her own identity impacting her ability to do what she did? What you should be doing in the times you find yourself in? Are there any prophetic words or key scriptures you need to pull out again and go over?

Declare
What will you declare about your current time and season?

Reflect
Reflect on those in your sphere of influence who always seem to know the times and what to do in them. What characteristics mark them and their lives? What could you do to cultivate these characteristics in your life?

O Lord, revive Thy work in the midst of the years,

In the midst of the years make it known.

Habakkuk 3:2

12. Revival

What is your definition of revival? What do you hear when you read this verse in Habakkuk?

The definition of revival has varied over the years. For some, it is a reference to large numbers of people turning to Jesus as their Lord and Savior. The Welsh Revival, which took place from 1904 to 1905, fits that description. Some cultures or churches have used revival as a word to describe a meeting that becomes a series of meetings, perhaps lasting for a week or longer.

My desire is that we do not create definitions that limit our prayers or expectations. If we tie our understanding of the apostolic and revival together, we expand the meaning, and our own expectation, well beyond a series of meetings or even multitudes coming to faith in Christ.

As far as definitions are concerned, I am using two. The first one I heard on a podcast from Mark Sayers and John Mark Comer: "Revival is when Renewal goes viral." I particularly like this as it connects the personal encounter with God to the fruit of that encounter: impacting the world around us. It connects salvation, inner healing, sonship, and revival together.

The other definition creates an important connection as well: When one to millions of people come into a personal relationship with Jesus Christ—His person, His power, His presence, and His principles—then it must lead to change or reformation in our world. Since Jesus is the first apostle, then according to this definition, those saved also become apostolic. The apostolic sends people out to transform the world or, to use another phrase, to expand the Kingdom. It contributes to reformation by its very nature. Populating Heaven is wonderful and essential, but revival must do more than that.

Since the apostolic is relational, it makes sense that revival through the lens of the apostolic ensures it will be passed to the next generation and beyond.

The sequence is, therefore, that a series of "revival" meetings can create renewal, salvations, and a fresh appetite for the things of God. Tasting and seeing is a great place to start. If that renewal spreads from the individual to multitudes, then we have the next step. And if that next step is apostolic in nature, then it should lead to reformation. Finally, if the apostolic can grasp true success and succession planning, then it will pass to the next generation.

The apostle is relevant to the equipping of the saints through each of these stages. Not only that, but the remainder of the fivefold find their place as well, especially if they have become apostolic in their approach to pastoring, teaching, prophesying, and evangelizing. And it doesn't stop there; the saints become trained and equipped for the work of ministry which extends beyond the walls of the church into every sphere of influence and realm of our world.

You cannot and should not attempt to separate revival from the apostolic. An apostolic revival will bring Heaven to earth, see multitudes saved, lead to societal transformation, and be sustained and passed on to future generations.

Review
What is your definition of revival? How is revival different when influenced by the apostolic? Read about one of the well-known revivals (e.g. Asuza Street or the Welsh Revival) and identify markers of the apostolic in it.

Declare
What will you declare about revival and the role of revival in your own life?

Reflect
Consider revival in the context of your current areas of influence. What might revival look like in the world around you?

Then they will rebuild the ancient ruins,

They will raise up the former devastations,

And they will repair the ruined cities.

Isaiah 61:4

13. Reformation and Transformation

Before I begin to unpack this theme, I want to briefly address the question of using the word reformation or transformation. My personal preference is reformation as, for me, it expresses a desire to be reformed according to an original pattern, plan, and purpose. While using this term, I am very conscious that for some it has pain attached and can remind us of the great division caused by the reformation of Martin Luther. My hope is that we will be able to pursue the best of both words towards an outcome of Revelation 11:15: the kingdoms of this world becoming the Kingdom of our Lord and His Christ.

Much of the Church does indeed hear the word reformation and reflect back to over 500 years ago and the days of Martin Luther. Time has passed since then and many views and opinions of that event have been voiced. Regardless of our opinions, most agree that we once more need a reformation or transformation that impacts the Church, churchgoers, and the world in which we live and serve.

It is essential to my beliefs that this reformation unites the Church and transforms society. We have come a long way from the days of Martin Luther and benefit from many of his reforms. One outcome of his teaching, however, was a divided bride, and that is not what we need today.

My favorite outcome of that reformation was the end of the division between priests and believers. Martin Luther talked of the priesthood of all believers. He spoke in the context of the traditional practice of the priest leading and the choir singing in a different language to that of the congregants. The priesthood of all believers was a statement of unity, desiring that all should be able to enjoy and experience God together, in the same language.

That statement, and subsequent change, has taken us from seasons of hymns, scripture in song, Psalm praise, and praise and worship to our current experience of encountering the presence of God in worship. We are a blessed people to say that we can literally take our worship with us everywhere we go.

As we pursue another reformation, there is a related theme that is central to moving forward. In fact, it can be given the same title: The Priesthood of All Believers. This time, however, this theme is not about giving everyone access to participate in worship. Instead, the heart of this reformation is that everyone know that they are priests, whoever they are, whatever they do, and wherever they go. This is essential to a reformation that embraces the apostolic.

An apostolic reformation is a reformation led by an apostolic mindset of bringing Heaven to earth and expanding the influence of King Jesus and His Kingdom. It involves continuous changes in the Church as she embraces the assignment of bringing Heaven to earth, expanding the

Kingdom, and training and equipping people from every sphere of influence to bring change and transformation to their part of the world.

Four key transitions in the Church must take place for this apostolic reformation:

> *From pastoral first to apostolic first.*
> *From church first to Kingdom first.*
> *From Big Church first to "Big People" first.*
> *From control first to empowerment first.*

None of these four transitions mean that we won't still gather as a church and pastor people. Rather, the emphasis of our gathering must change to become more apostolic.

An apostolic reformation brings change to the Church, which in turn raises and sends sons and daughters to bring change to the world. As I have said elsewhere, reformation and revival must go together, flowing into each other.

So what is reformation, really? It is when the whole of society, regardless of their personal relationship with Jesus, comes under the influence of the person, the power, the principles, and the presence of Jesus.

> *Reformation leads to a transformed society and a united bride.*
> *Reformation unites the Church.*
> *Reformation empowers the true priesthood of all believers.*

Reformation centers around the life, death, and resurrection of Jesus.

Reformation affects and is accessible to every nation, tribe, and tongue.

Reformation displays the power and presence of God, and releases the daughters and sons of God into their full expression.

I'm sure there is more, but most of us would be delighted to see this list made manifest.

Review
Read the author's definition of reformation again. What might this look like in the world around you, were it to happen today?

Declare
What will you declare to reinforce what you have learned today?

Reflect
Have you noticed the trends in terms of worship in the church over the past few decades? If it is to continue to be reformed in an apostolic way, what changes do you see happening in the next ten years?

*You had the seal of perfection,
full of wisdom and perfect in beauty.*

Ezekiel 28:12

14. Renaissance

We were created by the Creator to be creative, and to use our creativity to point mankind back to the creator.

Many theologians consider Ezekiel's description of the King of Tyre in Ezekiel 28:11 to be a reference to Satan or Lucifer before the fall. In other words, God created Lucifer in beauty, but Lucifer, in turn, used beauty to draw mankind to himself rather than point them to the creator.

Interestingly, Ezekiel uses the same Hebrew word to describe the temple out of which a river flows (Ezekiel 43) as he does to describe the King of Tyre's beauty. The word used in the original Hebrew is *tokniyt*.

The meaning of the word *tokniyt* can be summarized as meaning full of wisdom and perfect in beauty. In other words, before the fall, this was how Lucifer or Satan was created; and the temple that creates a river is described using the same word. There is a connection between beauty and wisdom and the flow of the river—which, to me, represents revival.

What does this have to do with Renaissance?

Renaissance is a renewed expression of creativity, inventiveness, and innovation, which brings glory to God and advances the kingdom of Heaven on earth. Many know of the Renaissance typically referred to as the period from the fourteenth century until the sixteenth century or so, depending on whether you subscribe to a long or short historical version. Although the church and religion played their part in this season, so too did humanism, and the belief that man has expressed himself creatively without God. The Renaissance ended with an emphasis on secular humanism. What a tragedy when so much of the art, music, and other creative expressions declared, "To God be the glory." For some art historians, the seasons of the Renaissance are even divided according to the way in which Jesus was portrayed on the cross.

Today, we live in what can be described as a creative age. The endless opportunities and access to creativity are evidence of this. In so many areas of life, this generation that has been informed by excess is crying out for and pursuing art, beauty, creativity, and excellence. It is time for a new renaissance.

The connection between the apostolic and renaissance is, at its core, a simple one. Although renaissance touches many aspects of the apostolic, two stand out.

Firstly, apostolic renaissance raises a generation of people who are secure in their identity and know that the Father gives us the desires of our hearts. Stimulated by beauty, they believe that they can express themselves, discover, and invent in ways which will point man to God.

Secondly, the apostolic has unlocked us from the confines of ministry being solely in the church. We know that we are sent. It's time for dreamers, creatives, thinkers, inventors, and innovators to not just know who they are and what they are here for, but to be sent out to influence this world.

Bringing Heaven to earth is central to the apostolic. In the context of apostolic renaissance, that means bringing the beauty and creativity of Heaven to earth. I have taught many times on the river which flows from the temple as described in Ezekiel. Without going into the full extent of what I teach, my studies revealed an answer to the question: What kind of temple creates a river of revival? The answer I found in studying Ezekiel is that it is the temple that is full of wisdom and perfect in beauty. The temple can refer to a corporate gathering or to the individual. After all, we are all temples of the Holy Spirit.

It is time for the release of beauty, flowing from the temple and out into the world. Beauty is a powerful resource. Its ability to display goodness and truth is evident. More than that, it is waiting to be infused by Heaven, and bring Heaven's answers and solutions to earth's problems and challenges.

Of course, a renaissance is not just connected to the apostolic. There also exists a clear connection between renaissance and the prophetic and teaching. It is, however, the apostolic culture that has the ability to empower a generation to grab hold of a unique moment in history.

I am convinced that it is time for us to take our place, to not allow the inventors and innovators of our world to be those without a greater purpose of glorifying God and pointing man back to the originator of our creativity.

Review
What has been your experience of beauty? How has it impacted your world and pointed you to Jesus?

Declare
What will you declare over your life with regard to beauty, creativity, and renaissance?

Reflect
Being created by a Creator, you are creative! Being creative looks different for everyone. What does creativity look like for you? Spend some time on beauty and creativity this week.

As a wise master I laid a foundation, and another is building upon it. But let each man be careful how he builds upon it.

1 Corinthians 3:10

15. Building on the Foundation of Others

I recently visited the Sagrada Familia in Barcelona, a cathedral that has been under construction for over a hundred years. The cornerstone of the Temple was laid in 1882. A foundation was built, a design laid down, and now generations of craftsmen have built upon the original foundation. Those who designed the cathedral and laid the foundations will never see its completion. Yet every subsequent generation of builders is following a master plan.

The picture of Sagrada Familia is a helpful yet perhaps surprising one in our modern world. In a world where it is possible to build a billion-dollar business in a matter of months, it is difficult to get a sense of Paul's meaning in 1 Corinthians 3:10. God is a generational and universal God and He invites us to step into His big picture—His grand plan—both in time and scope. After all, the whole earth will be filled with the knowledge of the glory of God and He is the same, yesterday, today, and forever.

When it comes to the apostolic, I believe there is much for us to learn about how to build. As revivals occurred through history, many have resulted in new denominations. While there is nothing inherently wrong with this, it is what happens next that is the issue. The energy of the revival which birthed the denomination is later lost in routine. It then often takes those outside of that denomination to rediscover the value of the original revival experience. While this demonstrates the principle of building on the foundation of the previous revival, it comes at a cost: the loss of momentum.

We also have a history of rejecting former moves of God or their leaders if they ended in failure or a moral fall. Fortunately, this was not the case with Solomon, or we would be lacking a priceless foundation and inclusion in our Bible. Learning the value of building on foundations without stumbling over faults and failures is part of the way of the apostolic.

The apostolic carries a reproducing dynamic. Without the apostolic influence, the pastoral tends toward a replacement model. Reproduction builds on the foundation of others and finds its identity in fathers and sons. The two great examples of this are Jacob and Jesus. Neither of them had a replacement plan, both had a reproduction plan, although it may not have been articulated in that way.

The family business for example, although not as common nowadays, carries this same reproducing dynamic. Each subsequent generation builds on the foundation of the previous, sometimes over the course of hundreds of years.

Learning from those who have gone before us is not a new concept—it is the basis of history and theology. But learning to build and create momentum from previous foundations—the apostolic approach—requires renewed emphasis in our modern era.

History is full of testimonies, and we know from Revelation 19:10 that testimony becomes the spirit of prophecy. Building on the testimony of others is more than a natural progression, it has a supernatural dynamic. Seizing the victories of those who have gone before, and embracing them in our cry for the future, directs our focus to what God has done rather than what man failed to do.

The threads of history are extraordinary. The simple connections between the Azusa revival and the Welsh revival are staggering. The revival in Los Angeles was built on visits to Wales, the sharing of testimonies, and letters between the leaders. In more recent times, we have seen a similar connection between Argentina and Toronto.

There are great challenges in our world: individualism, post-modern tribalism, and nationalism, to name three. If we are not careful, all three will draw us away from the awareness of being part of something bigger than ourselves. They will draw us away from the full understanding—the big picture—required for global and timeless revival and renewal.

A key to building on the foundation of others is to honor the past. As we honor the past, we also honor apostolic mothers and fathers, and in doing so, we understand that this will bring life.

Review
Read 1 Chronicles 22:5-19. What stands out to you as you read about King David's attempts to set Solomon up well to take over the throne from him? Where have you seen intergenerational building (inside or outside of the Church) done well?

Declare
What will you declare about your own role in building on another's foundation and laying a foundation for those who follow you?

Reflect
What are the hallmarks of things that last from generation to generation? Look at the people around you who have recently taken on new positions. What can you do to help them succeed in areas where the foundation wasn't well laid?

Do not let the world squeeze you into its mold.

Romans 12:2 (PHILLIPS)

16. Overcoming Secularism

It seems sometimes that I was asleep for a decade or two, and while I slept, a secular mindset became the acceptable norm. The Church has come under increasing pressure to dial down its principles and either deny the supernatural or make it no different to the supernatural experiences or stories of our cultures. The pressure to stray from the ancient boundaries, principles, and truths that are the bedrock of the Christian faith is accompanied by the Church's attempt to be relevant in this changing world.

And here we are: caught up in political correctness, Christianity a minority group that is not given the same permission as other such groups, and the realization that merely stating the basics of our faith can have us accused of being "against," or "phobic," or "anti."

All of this has added up to hand us religion without relationship, Word without power, government without principles, creation without Creator, the created without guidance, beauty without purpose, and supernatural experiences lacking necessary discernment. The apostolic's great opportunity is to put these back. This is almost a complete summary of the apostolic assignment. To restore what is lost, we need a relationship with our Heavenly Father, Heaven's principles for living life, and the power to bring Heaven to earth.

The war on secularism is a subtle war. It is not as simple as finding the single source of the enemy and the direction of attack. It is about understanding the culture in which we live. I recently heard this definition of secularism given by Mark Sayers, of Red Church Melbourne: the desire to have the Kingdom's benefits without the King.

The truth of that is evident all around us. For example, the concept of "deconstruction" carries this sentiment. It is a rejection of church and construction of our faith as a necessary part of our Christian lives, with the argument that we can do church in other ways. One example is leaders walking away from their faith but declaring that we must still walk in love. This idea also includes the constant rejection of the principles and standards of the Christian journey, instead expanding the truth of loving the sinner to embracing the sin as acceptable. In the process, the deconstructing believer is encouraged that leadership and authority are an old way of leading. Leadership accountability is seen as unnecessary and just another tool used to control. This is what it can look like to desire Kingdom benefits without a relationship with the King.

Of course, there *are* problems with the church. It is not perfect and some churches have lost their way. Not all leadership carries at its center the heart of a son—that of a servant leader who lives to empower their people. And accountability has too often drawn its strength from enacting the law rather than empowering people to be all that they can be.

This is where the apostolic must find its place. Putting our relationship with a good Father God at the core of what we build is apostolic. That one endeavor will change the culture around us. The apostolic is built around culture, and it is cultural transformation that we need.

Putting our relationship with God first will also give us the correct motive for purity and the application of spiritual principles in our lives. The desire to walk as closely as possible to our Father, and to reveal His son Jesus to the world, will correct secular thinking and leanings in the same way loving my wife will ensure my walk of purity. As we put Him first, we see an increase in the evidence of the goodness of our creator Father. We become aware that the principles of the Garden of Eden and the Law were not the restrictions of a harsh, mean-minded, despot god, but of a loving Father who knows what's best for us, made us in His image, and gave us the Maker's instructions.

In this relationship, we get to walk in power. Not our power, but His, working through us for the benefit of mankind.

The Kingdom without the King can only be temporary. It is rooted in selfishness and in the here and now. Its philosophical roots are not new; we have been here in different forms throughout history.

We live in a world that has access to the opportunities of this material and globally activated era, enabling us to attain a version of Heaven on earth in our standards of living. Because of this, our words without power have nothing extra to offer the world.

But this is our time, our generation, and our stage. We are apostolic sons and daughters of the King, assigned to expand His Kingdom in relationship with Him, revealing the truths and principles He gave us for life here and for all eternity.

Let's put the plumb line back in place.

Review
Have you been tempted to pursue the "Kingdom without the King"? In what ways have you seen secularism creep into your sphere of influence?

Declare
What will you declare to reinforce what you have learned today?

Reflect
How can you put your relationship with a good Father at the center of everything you do and build? Ask God what changes you could make, and what it might look like to make these changes.

In order that by them you might become partakers of the divine nature.

2 Peter 1:4

17. An Apostolic Culture

Now that we know that apostolic is a mindset resulting from the influence of an apostle in your life, we need to see how that creates an apostolic culture. It's worth noting that an apostolic culture is not just relevant in the church, although that may be the place we first, and more commonly, experience it.

A simple definition of culture is "the way we do things around here." Culture includes the thoughts, traditions, beliefs, and routines of a people group. Creating culture must be intentional because we are surrounded by communities and organizations that have and create a culture of their own.

If you leave an organization or group of people alone, they will most likely develop earth's culture. Unwritten rules will be created which the leader did not initiate. In JB Phillips's now rarely used translation of Romans 12:2, he said, "Don't let the world squeeze you into its mold." It is truly brilliant as it recognizes that there is an earth-centered way of doing things. If we don't intentionally pursue the opposite—Heaven's culture—earth's culture will make us into its mold.

Culture can also be described as stories we tell ourselves about ourselves. We are Heaven-based beings with a Heavenly family and so it stands to reason that our stories should be pointing to or originating from Heaven, just like the parables or stories which Jesus told. Our apostolic stories carry the nature of God and create Heaven's culture around us.

So what is an apostolic culture? It is, quite simply, the culture of Heaven. In the absence of finding the word culture in the New Testament, Peter's statement (2 Peter 1:4) that we have become partakers of the divine nature is a good substitute.

An apostolic culture starts in the unseen. It is related to faith, the presence of God, supernatural interventions, and hope. The goal of the apostolic is to create a Heaven-based culture in which all of the fivefold gifts, in particular, can operate on earth from Heaven's perspective. The apostolic, for instance, lifts the pastoral gift up from being satisfied with relying on earth's natural resources and solutions to seeking the pastoral interventions of Heaven and the supernatural. But it doesn't stop there, it equips every believer to use their natural and spiritual gifts for Heaven's advantage, benefit, and glory.

Put simply, the goal of the apostolic is to intentionally bring, contribute to, and create Heaven's culture on earth.

Here is a basic set of steps to creating an apostolic culture:

1. *I am influenced by an Apostle*
2. *I am apostolic*
3. *I behave differently*
4. *I create an apostolic culture around me*

To set an apostolic culture in place, you don't have to be an Apostle—you just need to have one in your life. Ideally, we will find ourselves in a culture led by an Apostle, but if we don't, then we don't have to wait before we get started on creating an apostolic culture. We are all led by the first Apostle.

As we saw already, Jesus is the first Apostle. This means that we need to have an understanding of the aspects of Jesus that are distinctly apostolic (more on this later). Fundamentally, the apostle is a "sent one." Jesus was sent from Heaven to make earth like Heaven, and He also sent us (John 17:18 and John 20:22).

Culture's power is most evident in relationships and interactions with other people. This is where all of us have the opportunity to create Heaven's culture. From our one-on-one relationships, to home and family, friend groups, workplaces, and on to those we may lead or the organizations we build, our privilege is to carry Heaven with us in stories, behaviors, routines, and principles.

Creating an apostolic culture involves storytelling, especially stories which reinforce faith, healing, and experiencing the presence of God—all of which infuse hope into the environment. These stories or testimonies create a prophetic atmosphere. People hearing these stories have their faith activated and believe that they too can see and experience these miracles in their own lives.

From stories and sharing the beliefs of the apostolic, behaviors are embraced. They are articulated, demonstrated and replicated. It is in this that "the way we do things around here" emerges. Stories carry beliefs, beliefs encourage behavior, and repeated and replicated behavior is the substance of culture.

Start simply. It is essential that you do not bombard your environment with too many cultural statements. They really are caught rather than taught, and the identification of three to five key cultures for your environment will enable everyone to recognize them as they are talked about, demonstrated, celebrated, and repeated.

For example, you will not go far wrong with creating a culture of the goodness of God, the presence of God, hope, healing, and miracles. Heaven is filled with the awareness of His goodness and the God of all hope is there, and there is no sickness.

Additionally, it is important to pursue cultures which serve the apostolic vision unique to your work, organization, or ministry. As we grow in understanding culture and how it helps us, we will see how to use it to serve our season, circumstances, or vision.

The apostolic automatically gives us vision often derived from the Apostle's foundational partner, the Prophet. But it must also be a vision derived from being sent. Culture serves the vision, creating the good soil in which the vision can be achieved.

Finally, in creating an apostolic culture, don't be afraid of repeating yourself. In fact, you must. If you don't have stories of your own yet, borrow some and look for people and situations where you can celebrate Heaven's apostolic culture on earth. Your goal is for everyone to "get it," carrying it into every aspect and relationship of your life and from there, taking it out to everywhere you have influence.

Review
As you look across your sphere of influence (home, work, church, etc.), what three to five key cultures are most important to you? What culture does your environment most need?

Declare
What will you declare to reinforce these cultures?

Reflect
What stories run through your sphere of influence?

But we all, with unveiled face beholding as in a mirror the glory of the Lord, are being transformed into the same image from glory to glory, just as from the Lord, the Spirit.

2 Corinthians 3:18

18. Change

It is now nearly thirty years since I attended my first Change Management workshop. I was working in a prison for young offenders and we had appointed a change management consultant as a result of serious national concerns regarding the standards of care. The management team and trade union representatives went away and gathered for two weeks, working through the prison's challenges. I confess to immediately enjoying it. I returned from that workshop appointed as the Change Manager, and so began several years leading workshops for prison staff. Little did I know that it would be a theme for the remainder of my life, both in prison and in the church, as well as the wider expression of bringing the Kingdom of Heaven to earth.

Change is not always well received by the church. "We've always done it this way," is a phrase I've heard more than once. At times, leaders justify this phrase by pointing to scripture that says God is the same yesterday, today, and forever. Yes, He is, but we must change to become more like Him and bring Heaven to earth.

While we often see change as an enemy, it is actually our mandate. Our initiation into the family of followers of Jesus began with change—our own personal transformation—and should continue with us bringing change to the people around us and the world in which we live. The language of the Bible even supports this idea of embracing change: redeem, return, rebuild, repent, recover, and reconcile are just a few examples.

The apostolic assignment is Heaven on earth; we are to expand the influence of King Jesus throughout the earth. Rather than an enemy or an interference, change is our assignment, our DNA, our modus operandi, and our raison d'être. It is our great privilege to be ambassadors of Jesus Christ at a time when the constantly changing world needs Heaven on earth more than ever.

What I learned at the change management workshop contained biblical principles, although the methodology needed aligning. I learned in those early days to discover what was wrong within an organization and try to fix it with a strategy. It is a method, however, which focuses too much on failure and weakness. My preferred approach is to look at what is right and help the organization to do it again. Remember, "The testimony of Jesus is the spirit of prophecy" (Revelation 19:10). We have been changed (our testimony) to bring change (prophecy).

As I reflect back on that first excursion into change management, I remember returning and talking to my pastor. I talked of the need for clarity of purpose and vision within the church. I knew instinctively and intellectually that change belongs to us. Every organization on earth is experiencing a moment of change: visional transition, missional transition, structural transition, and cultural transition. This also applies to the church. Two of the church's greatest transitions are shifting from gathering first to sending first, and from church first to Kingdom first. Unfortunately, I was not as well received as I hoped! Perhaps I was a little ahead of myself.

As Christians, we should be masters of change. We are, after all, the sent ones, sent to bring Heaven to earth. What greater change can there possibly be? It is the nature of the apostolic.

So how do we embrace change? Beginning a change journey with the desire of Heaven to see the testimonies repeated is a powerful starting point.

Review
Write out the key testimonies that you would like to see repeated. What can you do to see these testimonies happen again?

Declare
What will you declare to reinforce what you have learned today?

Reflect
Reflect on the phrase "Change is our assignment." How have you reacted to change? Have you been inclined to see it as an enemy or a friend?

From whom every family on earth derives its name.

Ephesians 3:15

19. Relational Government

From the beginning of the Bible to the end, there is a theme of family. It has, at times, been overlooked and even misunderstood. The act of removing Adam and Eve from the garden, for example, has been seen as punishment rather than a part of God's redemptive plan for His created family. In reality, God was ensuring that man was not eternally lost and that there was a way back to redemption. I often sum up the redemptive theme of the Bible in one phrase: God wants His kids back!

The illustrations of family in scripture are endless and beautiful. Perhaps we shouldn't be so surprised; our God is the Father from whom every family on earth derives its name (Ephesians 3:15).

Not only is family the expected outcome of our relationship with God, it is through family that this plan of Heaven will be achieved, and the structure from which it flows. It is not merely a theme to practice but a core principle to live out, potentially affecting every area of life and work.

For a long time we have described the church as a family, with many churches even including the word family in their name. We rightly talk about family because Heaven's original structure is family. Over time, however, we've often built or developed something else.

Outside of the church, we see that many organizations work to create a family environment in the workplace, not necessarily leaning on a biblical foundation for it, but still recognizing its value.

Within the church, that reality can easily be overtaken by building an organization, running programs, and developing management systems—all of which can gradually lose a relational focus.

We must remember that the apostolic is about bringing Heaven to earth, and that also includes the relational government structure of Heaven. Sometimes we limit our view of Heaven on earth to claiming what doesn't exist in Heaven shouldn't exist on earth. For example, there is no sickness in Heaven so there shouldn't be any on earth. But the reverse is also true. We should cry out for what *is* in Heaven to also be here on earth—and that includes government.

The good news about God's government is that He did not send a managing director or someone with a similar title representing control. The government of Heaven is on the shoulders of a Son (Isaiah 9:6), a wonderful counselor, mighty God, eternal Father, and prince of peace. The Father sent His son because He loved. He did not develop a scheme to manage man's failure and protect His own reputation. He sent love in the form of a son, who is fully God and fully man, so that His created kids could be restored in their relationship with Him.

Not only that, but the mankind they created was made in their image: the image of a family who ruled, created, expressed themselves, and together and forever pursue the restoration of family with everything they are.

This model must be our model as we co-labour with Heaven.

Heavens family exists in:

> *Perfection of love for each other in the trinity*
> *Perfection of honor*
> *Perfection of loyalty*
> *Absolute security in their own and each other's purpose*

In those four descriptions we have everything we need to model ourselves as members of Heaven's government on earth. We call it church, but the definition of the word we translate as church—ecclesia—is perhaps more accurately described as Heaven's local government office.

We see this in the culture Jesus created among the twelve He called disciples and apostles. We see Jesus at one point sending them out, seventy-two disciples in total. They went and saw many miracles, but when they came back, He told them what *He* saw. He talked of principalities falling as the disciples demonstrated Heaven's government. By sharing what He saw, He connected His small group to something bigger than themselves.

Jesus modeled family for three years. He did this by empowering, not limiting, by drawing them close so they could be sent out, by giving them grace to make mistakes, by allowing them to get caught up in the desire for greatness. The limitless one didn't limit those around Him, and nor must we. Jesus is the first apostle, His model is apostolic, and therefore the fruit of His discipling is apostolic. That looks like family.

A family government raises representatives who are sent to reproduce. Replacement is not the goal; neither of the two great models of government in the Bible replaced themselves—they reproduced themselves. This is the model of Heaven.

We are the adopted sons and daughters of the Royal Family of Heaven and, as such, we are also called ambassadors, representatives of another land or principality. Our assignment is family government. Together we have been given a vision of the future, and each one of us is invited to dream with that vision and to discover what part we play in seeing that vision come to pass.

Our assignment of making earth look like Heaven can only be carried out in the context of family—Heaven's relational government. The outcome of this assignment? An eternal family.

Review
The model of Heaven is family. What does this mean to you? What do you see in Heaven that you would like to see on earth?

Declare
What will you declare to reinforce the idea of Heaven's relational government in your life?

Reflect
Reflect on the characteristics of Heaven's family. How does replication differ from reproduction? What is created in a culture of reproduction?

Now concerning spiritual (supernatural) gifts, brethren, I do not want you to be unaware.

1 Corinthians 12:1

20. The Supernatural

Being sent from Heaven to change earth means that our assignment is twofold: to remove all things on earth that are not celebrated in Heaven, and to bring all things that are celebrated in Heaven to earth. Our assignment, therefore, must include the supernatural because there are things in Heaven that we cannot see here on earth. In fact, with God, everything is supernatural. Before creation, everything we can now see was once supernatural—it only existed in the heart and mind of God.

We are, as Peter writes in 2 Peter 1:4, "Partakers of the divine nature." A simple study of God's nature reveals that His manifold names include the supernatural. None are clearer or more important perhaps than Jehovah Rapha—the Healer. It is clear that we cannot do the works of Jesus, accept the assignment, manifest the divine nature, or bring Heaven to earth without embracing the supernatural.

Yet, generations of Christians have suffered from some church cultures embracing cessationism, which has taught that the miraculous and supernatural works of God have all but ceased, and they certainly don't flow through the ministry of men and women.

Remember, culture is created when we take something we believe and demonstrate that belief through our behavior. As I shared previously, culture is the word that describes "the way we do things around here." Religion has been described as "form without power." In other words, values and beliefs which are not lived out. Not only have some church cultures embraced cessationism, but we have also allowed heaven's culture to be reduced to a non-spiritual one by adjusting our theology to fit our experience on earth.

Our faith, our membership in this Jesus-commissioned family called the Church, is based on believing what we cannot see. That is the very heart of the supernatural, believing in things which we cannot see. Just because we have prayed for something and not seen the supernatural answer does not mean that God does not bring supernatural answers through our prayers. It means that we need to still apply faith, waiting and believing for that which we have yet to see. This is the very nature of faith.

The apostolic, likewise, is about bringing something we cannot see to a place where we can see it. The apostle will be defined as such if they embrace, pursue, and see the demonstration of the supernatural. In so doing, they will create an apostolic culture.

A friend recently shared about the success of a particular ministry. In describing it, he said that it succeeds because the leaders and members know their "superpower." While that is an uncomfortable word, it sums up what happens when we walk in the supernatural.

Many describe Christians as being supernatural beings (seated in Heavenly places) with a temporary residence on earth. Our nature, assignment, and gifts must, therefore, be supernatural. It begins with believing in resurrection, continues as we believe in the power to be saved and forgiven, then expands as we have faith for what we cannot see: pursuing healings, miracles, and prophecy.

Jesus said, "When I return, will I find faith?"

The answer then remains: will He?!

Review
Make a list of the names of God. Which ones contain the supernatural in some way? What does this tell you about who God is?

Declare
What will you declare to reinforce what you have learned today?

Reflect
To what extent do you rely on the supernatural to live the life Jesus has called you to? Look back over supernatural breakthroughs you have seen.

The whole earth will be filled with the Knowledge of the Glory of God.

Habakkuk 2:14

SECTION 3: APOSTOLIC LEADERSHIP

21. The Marketplace

Perhaps one of the great shifts in an apostolic culture is that the marketplace and serving in society becomes a valid mission field for the believer.

The pastoral model focuses on gathering, and often creates an expectation of attendance at church and upward promotion through the ranks of volunteers, deacons, and elders. There is nothing wrong with that, so long as we place value on the day-to-day ministry in the marketplace.

The apostolic, on the other hand, focuses on sending, and is directly linked to seeing His Kingdom come, on earth as it is in Heaven. Not, please note, in church as it is in Heaven. Although, if you get the earth, you will also get the church.

Within the apostolic culture, we have the great privilege of seeing Christians find fulfillment in every legitimate career and occupation. This is not a new theme, it has occurred many times in history, starting with the people of Israel for whom work was worship. In fact, there are few examples in the Bible of what we often call "full time ministry." Even Paul supported himself as a tent maker while also ministering the gospel, and he is by no means alone in this.

The reformation of society, for which we pray, requires a true apostolic emphasis of sent ones fulfilling their Kingdom purpose of bringing Heaven to earth. However, as ministry extends into the marketplace, one danger of the apostolic is the temptation to appoint marketplace apostles. In my opinion, this is misguided. Ephesians is clear that the five gifts are gifts to the church for the equipping of the saints for the work of ministry. The apostle equips the marketplace worker. My concern in appointing marketplace apostles is that we are in serious danger of creating a secular/sacred divide at a higher level. It would also tend towards the most successful Christian in any sphere becoming the "apostle" without necessarily being apostolic in their thinking and behavior.

What we need, therefore, is apostolic doctors, nurses, teachers, receptionists, computer operators, government leaders, artists and so on. We need apostolic believers who know that they are sent into the marketplace to do the work of ministry.

When the teacher in the classroom, for example, carries an inner awareness that they are sent and legitimately represent Christ in their career (even though it will look very different than ministry on a Sunday in church), it empowers and frees them to greater accomplishments in their field of ministry.

I would also suggest that, as we become fulfilled in our career choice, we are more likely to want to contribute to what is seen as more traditional ministry within the church. Isaiah 61 provides some insight. It begins with the statement of anointing to set captives free and bind up brokenhearted people. "Because the Lord has anointed me to proclaim good news to the poor. He has sent me to bind up the brokenhearted, to proclaim freedom for the captives" (Isaiah 61:1). There is, perhaps, no more universal captivity than that of feeling second-class. In this context, that captivity exists when we do not believe our work is a first class ministry. The truth is, perhaps only 3 percent of church goers are paid to go to church, which means that 97 percent find their income elsewhere. If the 97 percent feel less valuable, then we become a disempowered army of believers.

Isaiah 61 goes on to talk about the reversal of experiences and emotions for those once held captive. As the passage continues, it is the freed captives—not the anointed priest—who bring restoration to society. "They will rebuild the ancient ruins and restore the places long devastated; they will renew the ruined cities that have been devastated for generations" (Isaiah 61:4).

We go on to read that instead of shame, they receive a double portion and will be known as "priests of the Lord and ministers of our God."

These verses are so encouraging. Strangely, it seems so obvious, and yet, so often we have missed it. This passage has inspired me many times to pray commissioning prayers over "ordinary" churchgoers, and send them out as glory carriers—whoever they are, whatever they do, and wherever they go.

The apostolic creates an army of sent ones and the result is transformation. We need everyone to take their place, to use their skills, gifts, efforts, and anointing for the influence of the Kingdom of Heaven on earth.

Review
Has there been a sacred/secular divide in your thinking? The author says that believers are "sent into the marketplace to do the work of ministry." How does that shift your perspective toward your career or role?

Declare
What will you declare to reinforce what you have learned today?

Reflect
Reflect on the impact that being seen and encouraged can have, regardless of the sphere we are called to.

If the whole body were an eye, where would the hearing be?

1 Corinthians 12:17

22. Organization: The Sum of Many Parts

When we realize, as the Apostle Paul did, that the organization can be compared to the human body, we see that both embrace the following: The forces or properties which stimulate growth, development, maintenance, or change within a system or process.

Every one of you reading this book will in some way or another be connected to, or work within, an organization. Sometimes it is too easy to forget that we are part of something bigger than ourselves and that our contribution is vital. Part of that contribution is learning to steward our process or role within the context of the whole organization. I refer to the larger context—or parts—as dynamics.

Once we step into the realm of the apostolic, we will need to embrace an increased number of dynamics within our organizations—even if our organization is not church or ministry-based. We are no longer just stewarding the seen realities of the organization, but also the unseen realities of the Kingdom of Heaven.

What is important is for all of the dynamics to work together not allowing one to dominate. The unseen must work in partnership with the seen. Another way of looking at this is to view the dynamics of an organization as elements of the wine skin. Each has its place, but when one element consistently works without relationship with the others, it will make a rigid or torn wineskin.

A great verse which adds to this is Ephesians 4:16. This verse clearly tells us that the purpose is the whole body, but there are many joints, different elements which are provided by each part, and different ways of working which result in the building up or success of the whole.

While this is not an exhaustive list, there are at least twelve dynamics at work within an organization, each of which has a different purpose or operating system:

1. Supernatural — **Powerful** outside of our ability

   Common Problem: Relying on what man can do

   Key Diagnostic Question: What is your strength in this area?

2. Managerial enabling maintenance, progress, & support of leadership — **Purposeful** systems

   Common Problem: Lack of value for management systems

   Key Question: In which areas do you need more management systems?

3.	Organizational	**Practical** arrangements
	Common Problem:	Structure seen as inflexible or even unbiblical
	Key Question:	In what ways are you organized for victory?
4.	Leadership spirit & vision leader	The **Face & Father.** The culture
	Common Problem:	Top down control
	Key Question:	Are we a Boss- or Dad-led organization?
5.	Creative Expression	**Beauty & Inventiveness that glorifies God**
	Common Problem:	Beauty can be seen as cosmetic, an extra, an extravagance
	Key Question:	Is our expression ugly, tired, and dated or beautiful, alive, and current?
6.	Strategic	**Positioning** for the future
	Common Problem:	Failure to plan, "only led by the spirit." Same ol' same ol', stuck.
	Key Question:	Where will we be in five years if we don't plan?

7.	Relational	Connected as **Family by Honor**
	Common Problem:	Disconnected, relationship not seen as priority
	Key Question:	Who is genuinely asking me and who am I genuinely asking, "How are you?"
8.	Transformational	Bringing **Change** on purpose
	Common Problem:	Driven by change, not driving it
	Key Question:	Is change our enemy or friend?
9.	Spiritual	The unseen **resource of His presence** with and in us
	Common Problem:	A natural/spiritual division in tasks and roles
	Key Question:	Is there room for the spirit's prompting in the most practical of meetings?
10.	Professional	**Competence** and **qualification**
	Common Problem:	Lack of acknowledgement that professionals, (accountants, lawyers etc.) have to adhere to rules and guidelines as they serve the

		spirit and the external world.
	Key Question:	Are the professionals included in the spiritual activities?
11.	Prophetic	Encountering our **God who knows our future**
	Common Problem:	Getting dusty on a shelf
	Key Question:	What prophecy do you most want to see fulfilled?
12.	Communication	Flow of **Information** in, out, and throughout the organization
	Common Problem:	Getting stuck in the bad news and problems
	Key Question:	Is there more good news than bad?

Every dynamic is meant to serve the organization, as well as honor and show value for the other dynamics. As they work together, they should each express the spirit of the organization.

The hospital administrator, for example, must pay as much attention to the goal of health and healing as the surgeon or physician. That is the spirit of a hospital. The inventory manager of a warehouse must focus on the spirit of excellence and customer support as much as the sales team and the CFO.

When it comes to a more obviously supernatural environment, this is why the administrator must be familiar with the power of God. If they are not, then they will reduce a move of God to what man can do without God.

Ask yourself how each dynamic—or at the very least, the one you are most familiar with—is serving or impeding the spirit of your organization. An organization is the sum of many parts. You, sent one, are an important part, serving the greater spirit and vision of the whole.

Review
What is the spirit of your organization? Which of the twelve dynamics of an organization strikes you? What does God want to tell you about it?

Declare
What will you declare to reinforce what you have learned today?

Reflect
Choose one of the twelve dynamics and imagine what it could look like in your culture over the next five years if that dynamic expressed the spirit of your organization.

And God has appointed in the church, first apostles, second prophets, third teachers, then miracles, then gifts of healings, helps administrations, various kinds of tongues.

1 Corinthians 12:28

23. The Apostolic and the Gift of Government (Administration)

If ever a subject was found in a surprising context, it would be administration, or—as it's called in some translations—government. In Corinthians, Paul places it with apostles, prophets, miracles, and healings. In this context, the gift of government/administration is elevated by association.

I am convinced that we need this gift more than ever, which is why I teach on this subject. The gift of administration is often viewed as less spiritual, yet it is still a gift. Like the other gifts, it is meant to be infused with Kingdom purpose, empowered by supernatural thinking, and used to bring Heaven to earth. If we view the gift as less spiritual or valuable, we are in great danger of viewing the minister of that gift in the same way.

Three themes come together as we consider the gift of administration in the context of an apostolic move of God.

Awareness of the power of God: A move of God must sustain its dependency on the supernatural power of God. The administrator who does not understand and access the power of God will reduce a move of God to what man can do without God. This is the routinization of revival. Without that awareness of God's power, we disconnect from mystery, divine order, tension, and the realization that there is always more. I have taught much more on this in my series, Mastering Kingdom Administration.

Experiencing the presence of God: It is in the presence that we often gain an understanding of God's value for the work of our hands. Moses experienced the presence and from that place was commissioned to build a house for God. Instead of holding a rod and seeing a tabernacle miraculously appear, Moses was instructed to select skilled men and women and their resources to complete the project. If the administrator does not experience the presence of God, they will not understand the value that God has for their work.

Experiencing sonship: An administrator, manager, CEO, or church leader who is not a son will eventually lead by fear and turn an empowered culture into a culture of control. The son who is secure in his identity will continually empower his team and workers, knowing that it is only in the culture of freedom and empowerment that there is potential for ongoing increase.

We must learn to see and embrace the gift of administration at its highest level in every organization and move of God. Administrators steward the vision—serving the overall mission. The highest level administrator of a nation is the one who sets the vision, represents the nation as a father or mother, and recruits the team to get the nation to the destined vision. It is not the gift of helps, it is a servant gift, yet not a gift for servants but leaders. It is also the gift which holds together the five gifts.

I often view this as the hand: five fingers all joined, all connected, all dependent on each other, able to work together and individually. At other times, I see the gift more like the commander in chief in the United States. The president embraces this title in times of war, when he moves into the command suite and works with the joint chiefs of staff. The president is not the expert, but rather the hand, ensuring that each one plays their part, and that they are connected together for a greater purpose. It is the language of Ephesians 4:16: "From whom the whole body, being fitted and held together by that which every joint supplies, according to the proper working of each individual part, causes the growth of the body for the building up of itself in love."

The apostolic and the gift of government are inseparable. After all, the government (Isaiah 9:6-7) is on the shoulders of a Son and He is the apostolic one.

Review
How have you viewed the gift of administration? As boring, or life-filled? As the job of a secretary, or of a leader?

What can you do to expose those who are responsible for administration in your culture (which may be you!) to sonship, the supernatural, and the presence of God?

Declare
What will you declare to reinforce your understanding of the connection between the apostolic and administration?

Reflect
Where do you see the power and presence of God highlighted in the culture you are building?

With a view to an administration suitable to the fullness of the times, that is, the summing up of all things in Christ, things in the heavens and things upon the earth.

Ephesians 1:10

24. Structure and Organizational Leadership

The word translated as "administration" in Ephesians is a different word than that used in 1 Corinthians 12:28. The word used in Ephesians is related to stewardship or management of a household.

During my transition from prison management to church-based ministry, I began to notice some church leaders refer to organization, structure, management, and administration with a degree of disdain. It was a new experience for me to hear leaders of organizations talk in this way. They were mostly subtle comments, but they got my attention and caused me to question some of my training and experience. In that process, I realized it was time to learn how to marry my training and life experience with the church world in which I found myself immersed.

In 2005, two years after I transitioned to church-based ministry, my senior leaders gave me a new assignment—to build a relational network of leaders and churches. To give you some context, these are leaders who are well known in some of the most charismatic streams in the world. Imagine my pleasure when I was commissioned to this new assignment with the following statement: "It is all about the wine. The wineskin's purpose is to receive, carry, and pour out the wine in whatever form He comes tomorrow." These words were music to my ears. The wineskin is a biblical description of organization.

In the natural world, it is unthinkable that a winemaker would not value the structures that hold the wine: tanks, barrels, bottles, wineskins. Without them, wine cannot be made, stored, carried, or poured out. It is also unthinkable that a winemaker would bypass the making of wine barrels and send out for some plastic containers from his or her local supplier just to save a little money. Rather, she would know that there are particular trees that produce a particular wood that she will go to great lengths to access because of their effect on the process of winemaking.

Equally, a wine barrel maker would most certainly have knowledge of wine, how the barrel affects the wine it holds, and even have an opportunity to taste the wine. Put simply, the wineskin maker must not only know wine, but also understand the effect that the storage container has on the wine at every stage.

What does this mean for us? It must be the same with the building of systems and structures to receive, carry, pour out, and store the wine of revival, refreshing, and renewal. We must understand what the structure and systems are intended to carry and pour out. If we don't, then we will most likely build a bureaucracy: a structure that serves structure itself.

With our increased awareness of the new and ongoing outpourings of the Holy Spirit, and with a fresh awareness of creativity and its purpose, we must embrace more than just an organizational chart and a strategic plan. We must embrace the understanding that the very essence of a supernatural and creative move of God is related to a value for organization and administration.

This is vital both in the church and outside of it. My passion to erase the secular/sacred division reaches a crescendo here. Inside the church, the administrator is often given a less spiritual title and even kept out of the "spiritual" meetings. On the other hand, outside the church, the most valued qualification for an organizational leader is a Master of Business Administration. Yet, within the church, these same people often find themselves less valued for these very real qualifications. It is a dilemma which must end. We need great spirit filled administrators working in the church and in every sphere of influence.

As apostolic wineskin makers—or organization leaders—we live in tension. It is all about the wine, the Holy Spirit, and the purpose of the organization. Yet, without the wineskin or wine barrel, the wine is wasted. With an inferior wineskin, the wine is spoiled. Both have catastrophic consequences.
In other words, the mistakes we make fall into two primary categories: we reject the role of the wineskin entirely, deciding to be led by the wine (Holy Spirit) and missing the truth that wine needs a wineskin; or we focus so heavily on the structure of the wineskin, that it becomes useless to the outpouring of a new type of wine.

Structure and systems have great purpose. Take the human body, for example. Remove the skeleton, and we are in trouble.

Remove everything but the skeleton, and we have the dry bones of Ezekiel. We live in days of extraordinary change and Kingdom Administration is the gift needed to steward that change. Being able to receive, carry, and pour out tomorrow's innovations and modes of operation is essential to future success.

Competitors are everywhere and they don't take generations to capture the market. But equally problematic is to be so focused on new innovations that proper time is not given to the builders who will design, build, and maintain the innovations. There needs to be a balance of innovation and structure. We need to both understand the wine and have value for the wineskin.

The apostolic always has a destination, a purpose, a vision, and a goal. That is also the language of administration. However, all of those things—destination, purpose, vision, and goal—require a means, or a "how." How is the structure, the organization, the vehicle used to bring the outcome.

Review
Look into the process of winemaking and specifically the making of wineskins and barrels. What insights do you find into the stewardship of revival and the apostolic?

Declare
What will you declare to reinforce what you have learned today?

Reflect
Have you been guilty either of rejecting the wineskin for the wine, or of rejecting the wine for the wineskin? Reflect on the statement, "It's all about the wine," and ask God to speak to you as you do so.

And do not forget to do good and to share with others, for with such sacrifices God is pleased. Have confidence in your leaders and submit to their authority, because they keep watch over you as those who must give an account. Do this so that their work will be a joy, not a burden, for that would be of no benefit to you.

Hebrews 13:16-17

25. Accountability

When I found myself in what I prefer to call "career church ministry," I started to review management practices from my nursing and prison careers. In those worlds, management was the norm, but, as I mentioned previously, that was not the case in my new environment. Some of these management practices included job descriptions, annual staff reports, staff disciplinary systems, and personnel or human resource management. Reviewing these in light of an apostolic culture led me to see that these practices, while still very much needed, require a different approach to fit the culture.

The apostolic empowers. Alongside encouraging character growth, it also encourages self government as a fruit of the Holy Spirit. In the context of our assignment—bringing Heaven to earth, representing Jesus, honoring and calling out the greatness in each other, fostering a culture of dreams, and serving the Father's vision—the empowering nature of the apostolic creates a foundation from which to lead, manage, and be led and managed. This foundation is the different approach I was looking for.

Accountability—or in the case of management practices: disciplinary systems and personnel management—takes on a new emphasis in the context of the apostolic and its empowering nature.

As we embrace honor, accountability's first aim is that you be the best you that you can be. In other words, the first thing is to celebrate what is right, followed up by correction. We are, after all, significant, made in the image of God and invited to co-labour with Him. Punishment and control are not the approaches of our heavenly Father and His son Jesus. Quite the opposite. Jesus, in His death, took our punishment, did everything required for the restoration of relationships, and told us that we would see greater works. This is the mindset of restoration, redemption, and increase; not punishment and control.

I have already referred to the principle outlined by C.S. Lewis, "If you put second things first you will get neither first nor second. But if you put first things first you will get first and second." If we put correction first when it comes to accountability, then celebrate what is right second, we get neither the first nor the second. Instead we get punishment and control.

Accountability in an apostolic culture is not about first recognizing what is wrong with someone, but identifying, encouraging, and calling out what is worthy of praise. Using our Kingdom language of being "on fire" for Jesus, I like to view it this way: accountability is not that I make sure that you don't smoke (cigarettes), but rather that I make sure you burn (are on fire for Jesus).

The shift in thinking is that the individual is now responsible for their behavior and attitude, and the manager is the guide and encourager. This approach also extends into management of situations where there is failure. The first task is to get the person to take responsibility for their behavior and attitude (empowerment). From this place of ownership, the next conversation is much easier, as the question becomes, "How can I help you to be the best you that you can be?"

Rather than punishment for breaking rules, within this approach exists the potential for redemption, so long as the person takes responsibility, changes the way they think, and submits to the process of restoration. This process of accountability also requires a change in perspective by the guiding manager or leader. He or she must lead from the heart of the Father, accessing Heaven's view of the person, as well as a sense of their prophetic potential and purpose.

Similar approaches apply to job descriptions and annual staff reports. Job descriptions are an expression of the way in which we are invited to serve. While we may not all work for a church or an apostolic organization, we do all have a choice as to how we position our hearts toward our work. One key way to bring Kingdom insight into management practices is to see our work as a legitimate expression of our ministry here on earth. There is no sacred/secular divide. With that in mind, job descriptions become tools for organizational and personal success.

Equally, when approached from an apostolic perspective, the annual staff report becomes a record of our performance. I suggest that the report is more appropriately called an appraisal; it is an opportunity to give praise and encouragement for a job well done.

As we embrace all of the elements of an apostolic organization, it is easy to see how an apostolic approach to management practices compliments the culture and serves to bring increase. They become a source of life rather than another management task.

> *Accountability becomes giving an account for our growth and development.*
> *Staff reporting becomes an opportunity to be given praise and encouragement.*
> *Staff discipline becomes an opportunity to overcome weaknesses and even failures and progress along the journey of becoming the best version of ourselves that we can be.*

This is the apostolic way. The people we lead should benefit from our leadership. They should be encouraged in their contribution, grow in self belief, overcome weaknesses, and become the best expression of themselves that they can become.

One of my favorite examples of this was a situation where I was addressing a major failure by a member of my team. We had met several times and got to the point of understanding the circumstances. It eventually became clear that it would not be possible for him to keep his job. At the final meeting, when I told him that he was losing his job, he asked me for something which took me completely by surprise. This man, whose marriage had just ended and who was in the process of being fired—an event that could easily create a volatile reaction—asked me for a father's blessing. His explanation was that that experience was the best treatment he had ever received from an employer. I did as he asked and prayed a blessing over him, hugged him, and said my farewell. I will never forget that moment. It proved to me, beyond doubt, that the apostolic culture is capable of giving a positive experience in even the most challenging of scenarios.

Ultimately, what we need to remember is this: the key question and mindset underlying apostolic human resource management and accountability is, "How can I help you to be the best version of you that you can be?" It applies throughout the organization as well; to recruitment, appraisal, discipline, and even promotion.

Review
Take a look at the internal processes of your organization or even just your role. What could you change so that it is more closely aligned with an apostolic model of accountability?

Declare
What will you declare to reinforce your understanding of apostolic accountability?

Reflect
Reflect on your approach to issues among those you lead. Do you tend towards a disciplinary or empowering model in the way you deal with failure and success? How can you implement your answers to the "Review" portion of this chapter?

It was for freedom that Christ has set us free.

Galatians 5:1

So then you are no longer strangers and aliens, but you are fellow citizens with the saints and are of God's household.

Ephesians 2:19

26. Empowerment and an Apostolic Culture

"It was for freedom that Christ has set us free." The life, death, and resurrection of Jesus Christ led us from the Old Testament law-based culture to the New Testament culture of freedom. The external was replaced by the internal, and the assignment turned from Israel to the whole of humanity.

It is, however, essential that we understand the nature of this freedom. It is not a freedom to do what we like, rather, it is a freedom to experience all of the benefits previously limited to the people of Israel.

Ephesians 2:12 reads, "We were at that time separate from Christ, excluded from the commonwealth of Israel." Then, in verse 19, we read the following: "But you are fellow citizens with the saints, and are of God's household."

What a transition! We are now empowered members of the Royal Family of Heaven.

To empower, one needs something to give away. That something is power. It is impossible to empower someone unless you have power to give them.

An apostolic move of God is inseparable from empowerment. The very nature of the word apostolic—meaning "to send"—

implies setting free, empowering, trusting, or believing in someone.

The pastoral culture is focused more on gathering than sending, and tends, therefore, to create more controls. They are not necessarily wrong in their focus on gathering, but they are limiting themselves and others if control becomes the culture.

The illustration drawn from the life of Jesus is that He created a culture where the disciples argued about who was the greatest. This allowed a Judas to emerge. Jesus empowered those around Him to such an extent that these were the outcomes. Fear of repeating this, and raising another Judas, leads us to fear empowerment and freedom to the extent that Jesus demonstrated. While this may (or may not) help us avoid raising a Judas, it also prevents us from successfully raising world changers.

The apostolic is a sending culture and one where we give away power. We see this same essence of giving away illustrated through family in the "giving" of a daughter in marriage. This is not the evidence of control, but of freedom. It is a statement of permission to go and reproduce this family outside of the walls in which you have grown up. Family is, from the very beginning, apostolic in nature—empowering, sending, releasing, and reproducing.

With that in mind, an empowering leader:

Is first a son
Points to someone or something greater than themselves
Has a source of strength outside of themselves
Is not afraid of others surpassing them
Recruits people with different and stronger gifts than they themselves carry
Uses systems and structures to serve and to empower others

I love the story of Moses and his prayer for the people of Israel as they got closer to entering the promised land. It was the land that Moses would not enter despite a lifetime journey to get his people there. Moses' prayer was an empowering prayer, a giving and sending declaration. "Go in," he said, "take the land. May Heaven rain down dew on you and may your enemies fall before you." He empowered his people to go where he couldn't go.

What do you have to give away? Are there restrictions in your heart, or are you believing with Jesus that the ones that come after will see the greater works?

To empower others we must first have something to give, and it starts in our hearts. We may also have resources and actions to share, but to empower will always be a heart attitude first. It is also a two-way act. I love Bill Johnson's statement that he will not embrace someone's vision (in the context of his ministry) until he has seen that they have embraced his. This is the heart of a father who looks for the hearts of sons and daughters, and once they are aligned, begins to empower them forward.

Review
What does empowerment meant to you and what do you have to give away? How can you see yourself empowering those around you?

Declare
What will you declare to reinforce what you have learned today?

Reflect
Are there restrictions in your heart preventing you from going after the "greater works"? Ask Jesus where they came from, and work through what He shows you.

Our Father, who art in heaven.

Matthew 6:9

27. Apostolic Families

Two themes of Jesus are particularly important to understand. The first is relationships. It was Jesus who taught us to pray "Our Father," and that means that we are family. In fact, Paul writing to the Ephesians, went even further and described God as the one from whom every family derives its name. Jesus is the Son, sent by the Father, whose redemptive purpose is the restoration of all mankind to relationship with the Father. There is no strategy that reveals the importance of relationship more than this.

The second theme of Jesus is that in the same way He was sent by the Father, He sends us. John 20:21 says, "As the Father sent me so I send you."

Putting these two themes together, it is clear that we are family and we are sent (apostolic). Apostolic families should therefore be the description and model of the church.

What does that look like? The church should be a community that cultivates belonging, equipping, and sending. Some years ago, I developed a phrase that encapsulates what I was then trying to define: an Apostolic Resource Center. My problem was that I didn't really like the emphasis on resource. Resourcing is part of the apostolic, but it is not the whole, by any means. As I considered how to define this, I linked three aspects of the history of the church: a place of connection with God, belonging to a family, and going out into the world. The phrase or definition I then came up with to describe an Apostolic "Resource" Center was, "A community where people encounter God, become part of a family, and are trained and equipped to change their world."

When we resist the temptation to call church a place or a building, it becomes a community. It is meant to be a community of belonging, encountering, equipping, celebrating, and sending so that those who are a part of the bride of Christ have everything they need to bring about change and transformation in their spheres of influence.

Let's unpack those three key identifiers.

Encountering God includes:

> *Salvation: the ultimate and most important encounter.*
> *Healing: where we encounter His healing power.*
> *Worship: where we experience His presence.*
> *Intercession and Prayer: where we communicate with Him and for the needs of our world.*
> *Prophecy: where we encounter God, who knows our future.*
> *Inner Healing: where we are healed of the wounds of broken, absent, or abusive relationships and enabled to enjoy relationship with those around us and our glorious triune God.*
> *Revelation and the word*

Belonging to a family includes:

Shared origin and identity
Shared connection and value
Shared purpose and commitment
Shared future and dreams

Training and equipping to change the world includes:

Empowering every believer to discover and change their world
Equipping in the supernatural
Making disciples of the Kingdom

Of course, there is much more, but these provide a basis on which every church can build. I have yet to meet a church leader who does not want this simple phrase to describe their church: a community where people encounter God, become part of a family, and are trained, equipped and sent to change *their* world.

Every church, leader, and individual will find their particular emphasis of family. The encounters will look a little different, the evangelist will have a unique perspective, as will the pastor or teacher. But as long as they embrace the apostolic first, they will find their place in the family.

This model will create the diversity in the family of Christ that the world needs so desperately. It is not about us all being the same, but having unique encounters with God, being part of something bigger than ourselves, and carrying our unique expression with us everywhere we go, empowered by our experience in the community.

Review
Run through the list of encounters. Which of these have you experienced? How has each encounter blessed your life?

Declare
What will you declare to reinforce what you have learned about the importance of apostolic family?

Reflect
Read the Lord's Prayer. What aspects of apostolic family can you find within it? Consider the benefits of belonging and the importance of family. Do you find these concepts easy to embrace? Why or why not?

And on this rock, I will build my church.

Matthew 16:18

28. Big People

In Matthew 16, Jesus posed a question to his disciples: "Who do you say I am?" Peter responded, "You are the Messiah, the Son of the living God." Peter might not have realized it, but his acknowledgement of Jesus was the foundation for the rest of his life and ministry. Just a few verses later, in Matthew 16:18, Jesus' statement, "and on this rock…"served as recognition of Peter's stature in the Kingdom. I like to describe this stature as "big people." Big people, like Peter, know who they are and who He is.

The concept of big people begins with a shift in emphasis from the "man of God" to raising a body of people to represent the King and His kingdom, whoever they are, whatever they do, and wherever they go. The man of God culture, mindset, and behaviors are rooted in a secular/ sacred divide and probably go back hundreds of years. You will, by now, know that I honor the holders of office in the church, but their assignment is to equip, empower, send, and encourage *everyone* to bring change to their life and sphere of influence.

The underlying belief that there was only one "big" person, leading other less spiritual people, was, to be fair, not always the fault of the leader or organization in which they resided. The problem, however, is that if the church embraces the idea that ministry within the church is the highest calling, then the people attending either see success as achieving a position in the church, or they forever feel inferior in their career or role in life. Raising big people is at the heart of the apostolic and a focus of Ephesians 4. The goal of each of the fivefold is to equip the saints for the work of ministry. I have always interpreted the work of the ministry as including every legitimate career.

Creating a culture that raises big people is becoming a more common experience within the church thanks to renewed emphasis in some key areas. Inner healing and the teaching of sonship increases our confidence in our identities. Destiny teaching and coaching assist people as they pursue relevance in their lives and the world. Additionally, schools of supernatural ministry train people to bring Heaven to earth alongside the teaching of the seven spheres of influence. These emphases are raising big people.

As we see in Matthew 16, big people know who they are. The journey of sonship creates a strong foundation of identity. From that foundation, big people understand why they are alive, realizing they carry a sense of destiny of calling and vocation. Related to that, they have an expectation of the impact their life will have, and they know where they are going. Another way of summarizing this is that they are sons and daughters of destiny, who know how to bring Heaven to earth and expand the influence of the kingdom.

Once again, this is modeled by Jesus, who said many times who He was, why He was here, and where He was going. Perhaps most famously of all, He articulated in John 3:16 that the impact of His life would be access to eternal life for all mankind.

The nature of the apostolic embraces many elements: Identity, empowerment, and, of course, the apostolic itself. All of these help create the soil in which big people can grow. Bill Johnson continually communicates his desire to raise big people rather than concentrate on a big church. The reality is that if you get the former, you may very likely get the latter, but it doesn't work the other way around.

As a church, leading big people will change the vision and mission, affect the organizational structure, and require the creation of an empowering family culture. Most importantly, to *lead* big people, we need to be secure sons and daughters and lead from that place of security.

Review
Identify a few key people in your sphere who you could start to raise up and encourage on their journey.

Declare
What will you declare to reinforce what you have learned today?

Reflect
Have you experienced being part of a church or organization that builds big people, rather than focusing on building the organization? What were your experiences?

This Book of the Law shall not depart from your mouth, but you shall meditate on it day and night, so that you may be careful to do according to all that is written in it; for then you will make your way prosperous, and then you will]achieve success.

Joshua 1:8

29. Success or Succession?

In any organization, there is a need to develop a plan for future leadership. I suggest, however, that the emphasis on succession may not be the correct focus for us as apostolic leaders and organizations.

Succession tends to be connected with replacement, whereas success planning focuses on reproduction. Allow me to explain.

In an organization where the current leader is the founder, they are very often irreplaceable because they know everything there is to know about the company and have been involved in every aspect of the organization. When it comes time for them to step down, the question, "Who will replace me?" is the wrong one and may lead to compromise. While a new leader will need to be appointed, the idea of replacement can set the successor up for failure as they will lack major qualities or skills that the original founder carried and fulfilled.

For example, in an apostolic and prophetic organization, it may be that the founder had a high value and competence for both the apostolic and the prophetic. Yet, the chosen successor has not developed a value or competency for either. This style of succession planning can encourage an orphan heart in the one replacing and the one being replaced. If the founder is deemed "irreplaceable," then the successor simply cannot live up to expectations, leading to feelings of failure and fear of disappointing those they replaced.

Heaven's way is relational, which leads me to believe that Heaven's mandate is increase and multiplication. Families reproduce and multiply. It is the image of the single patriarch/matriarch creating several sets of future pairings.

Success planning, rather than succession planning, is based on being a son and desiring the next generation to go further. The family model also applies here, not just in terms of sonship, but in the fact that fathers typically have a number of sons and daughters. The idea of succession passes the torch to a single successor. But success planning focuses on the increase of the organization as a whole.

Success planning is also linked to an empowering culture, multiplication being the goal and result. There are two primary examples of Heaven's government in the Bible: Jacob and Jesus. These are significant examples of success planning because neither of them replaced themselves, they multiplied through their respective sets of twelve (Jacob's tribes and Jesus' disciples). The biblical and apostolic model in the Bible is also one of gathering for the purpose of dispersing and increase.

In many organizations, there will need to be a single successor, even with success planning. But the difference is, that successor does not need to replace, but rather reproduce.

Success planning begins with reviewing success, and, in particular, the culture which has underpinned that success. If the successor is given an understanding of the previous success of the organization in terms of culture and victories, then they are set up to build a team who will carry those elements forward under their unique leadership. In this way, the empowering culture of the previous leader gets reproduced, as does the spirit of the organization. That in itself leads to increase, which is the way of the apostolic and the goal of apostolic leadership.

Review
What are the successes of the organization you lead or work for? If these continued, what would success would look like in five years?

Declare
What will you declare today to reinforce your understanding of success planning?

Reflect
Reflect on a time when you've seen succession lead to decrease or unproductive change within an organization. What would it have looked like to focus on success over succession?

Greater works than these shall you do.

John 14:12

30. Maintaining Momentum

To be apostolic means that we are in submission to the commission of Jesus. That includes an almost all-embracing focus of the prayer which He taught us to pray, "On earth as it is in Heaven." We are to do this as part of a family—after all, the prayer begins, "Our Father...."

I want to highlight four ways of maintaining the apostolic as we continually walk lines of tension both between the promises of Heaven and the realities of earth, and the unity of Heaven's family with the realities of maintaining earth's relationships.

The challenge of maintaining what God has given us to do is by no means new. One of the greatest challenges in the Old Testament was sustaining, maintaining, and passing on the experiences of one generation to the next. Since the cross, history has shown us that sustaining and maintaining the apostolic and unity continues to be a great challenge.

There is a common organizational and generational pattern of losing momentum that is particularly evident in the church. In a faith setting, the pattern starts with those who find the fresh move of God, the outpouring, or revival. When it comes to the next generation, the focus of the outpouring often shifts to management. In the process, I suspect we become content, yet we are missing that which makes our faith, faith! This causes the impetus and energy of the original move of God to be lost, and it is not passed on to the third generation. That generation often has to go and discover it for themselves.

Why does this happen? We are often tempted to manage a move of God and reduce it to what can be seen and easily explained. The author Philip Yancey suggests that when we remove the supernatural element from our faith, we end up elevating the natural to a supernatural status. As I reflected on this, I became increasingly aware that in order to sustain the apostolic, there are certain elements of tension which must be kept alive.

First, a move of God needs to be stewarded in whatever form it comes, but always with the awareness of the power of God. If we don't embrace this tension, we are in danger of reducing a move of God to what man can do without Him.

Second, and equally important, is the matter of sonship and fathering. Our generation is in a great position regarding this, as we have been able to focus, perhaps more than any generation before us, on our identity as sons and daughters of the Father. Yet, Moses had this revelation thousands of years ago. While he was unable to go into the Promised Land and receive the reward of his life's journey, he blessed the people of Israel to go where he would not go. It was the act of a true son, who had become a great father. It is the same example Jesus gave us. He and the disciples had seen what most of us have never seen, and yet He blessed us to see and do greater works than even that.

These first two tensions are essential in maintaining the apostolic: the tension of bringing Heaven to earth, and the tension of blessing the next generation to go farther than we have gone.

Jesus embraced both of these elements when He told the disciples that they, and all who believed because of their words, would do greater works. He was releasing a mindset of belief that there is more and He was giving it to the generation who would run after Him.

The third tension that is necessary for maintaining the momentum of the apostolic is the pursuit of excellence. The pursuit of excellence is a lifestyle because excellence is a journey. We never arrive at a point of perfection, but we never settle for less than Heaven has promised.

Finally, the fourth element of maintaining the apostolic is success planning rather than succession planning. Instead of planning to replace the leader who was instrumental in the start of the move of God, we focus on repeating the success that we have witnessed.

So in summary, as we seek to maintain the apostolic we can:

> *Resist managing the life out of a move of God and instead maintain the tension between what is in Heaven and what we see on earth.*
> *Bless the next generation to go further.*

Pursue excellence (not perfection) and never settle for less than Heaven has promised.

Focus first on repeating the success of recent years rather than focusing on replacement of the leader who achieved it.

Review
Which of the four elements of maintaining the apostolic most resonates with you? What do you feel God is saying to you about it?

Declare
What can you declare of your own life and your church community with regard to maintaining apostolic momentum?

Reflect
Reflect on your belief systems. Is there any area in which you have watered down your beliefs to fit with your experience? What does God want to tell you about this?

But we also exult (rejoice) in our tribulations, knowing that tribulation brings about perseverance,
And perseverance, proven character;
And proven character, hope.

Romans 5:3-4

SECTION 4: EMBRACING AN APOSTOLIC LIFESTYLE

31. Perseverance

I am convinced that there is a deep connection between the apostolic and perseverance. While this may seem like an unusual theme, be encouraged, because the outcome of perseverance is hope.

It is significant to note that, before he wrote Romans 5, Paul lived out the realities of 2 Corinthians 11. Allow me to explain: Paul's letters do not appear in chronological order, but rather by virtue of their length. And so, we read in Romans (his final letter) chapter 5 this great sequence:

> *Exulting in our tribulations*
> *Knowing that tribulations produce endurance*
> *Endurance produces character*
> *Character produces hope*
> *And hope does not disappoint*

But before we can fully comprehend the enormity of these truths, we need to read 2 Corinthians 11. In those verses exist another list, the list of what Paul endured—and no doubt learned to exult in—before he wrote his final letter to the church in Rome. The list includes:

Hard labor
Imprisonment
Five times the thirty-nine lashes
Three beatings with rods
Being stoned
Being shipwrecked
...and more!

The word perseverance (or endurance, depending on your translation) in Romans 5 is translated from the Greek word *hupomone*. I reviewed a number of sources to discover that *hupomone* has an extraordinary meaning: The character of a man or woman, unswerved from their deliberate purpose and piety in life by even the greatest trials and sufferings. This is the place where hope is birthed. This idea of perseverance contains so much more meaning than just the ability to withstand hardship. It embraces the person, their purpose, and their character.

Another place we find perseverance is in 2 Corinthians 4:8-9. I particularly enjoy the Passion Translation for these verses. "Though we experience every kind of pressure, we're not crushed. At times we don't know what to do, but quitting is not an option. We are persecuted by others, but God has not forsaken us. We may be knocked down, but not out."

Paul says later, in 2 Corinthians 12:12, that perseverance is connected to the signs of the true apostle.

James also addressed this theme when he wrote in James 1:2, "Count it all joy my brethren when you encounter various trials, knowing that the testing of your faith produces endurance."

Peter, too, embraced perseverance when he spoke his last words (2 Peter 3:18) in what must be some of the finest advice of the Bible, if not history.

And finally, we see the theme emerge yet again when Hebrews 12:2 describes endurance in relationship to Jesus, "Who for the joy set before Him endured the cross."

This place of endurance, perseverance, pressing in, not staying down is not just the way of the Apostle, but also the way of the apostolic. If you are in a tough place as you read this, be encouraged. Hope is not birthed when everything is going well, but in *the ability to exult in the midst of troubles and difficulties.*

I want to suggest that the sent ones, the apostolic ones, do not quit—they endure, they press on. They may, at times, seem down, but they are not out. They are able to join Rocky from the movie of the same name in saying, "But it ain't how hard you hit. It's about how hard you can get hit and keep moving forward."

Perseverance is an attitude and character summed up so well by Saint Paul in Philippians 3:14 when he writes, "I press on." You only need to press on when there is resistance.

Be encouraged, fellow apostolic one, for it is in the enduring that your character is formed and reformed. Out of that place comes a gift of hope, which does not disappoint. Saying it does not disappoint is a confident promise, but it is true. Perseverance will always take you to the correct appointment as opposed to the wrong (dis) appointment.

As we bring Heaven to earth, the apostolic assignment will meet resistance. The good news is that same resistance, which can tempt us to quit, is the incubator of hope, and hope is related to faith; the faith to see signs wonders, and miracles.

Review
Read Romans 5. How do things change for you, knowing that the Apostle Paul wrote this passage after enduring such harsh treatment? How has "counting it all joy" worked out for you?

Declare
What will you declare in order to embrace the truth that perseverance leads to hope?

Reflect
Reflect on who around you needs encouragement to help them endure through to a place of hope. Take a step to encourage them today.

And to bring to light what is the administration of the mystery which for ages has been hidden in God, who created all things; in order that the manifold wisdom of God might now be made known through the church to the rulers and the authorities in the heavenly places.

Ephesians 3:9-10

32. Mystery

What is the administration of mystery? As someone with a passion for administration, Ephesians 3:9-10 has often attracted my attention.

Mystery is a familiar and significant subject that I particularly associate with my fifteen years at Bethel Church in Redding, California. None of us who were present will ever forget Bill Johnson teaching on the Sunday before his father passed. Many have since listened to that message and the one he gave the following week in a two-part series called "Enduring Faith." I commend it to you as one of the most powerful teachings on grief I have ever heard, only to be eclipsed in 2022 by another following the home-going of his wife, Beni Johnson.

Bill stood in front of us in January 2004 and made a statement that I usually paraphrase as: "God is Good. That is a Revelation. My father is dying of cancer. That is a mystery." He went on to say that he would not ever sacrifice the revelation of God's goodness on an altar of human reasoning to give an answer to a mystery. I remember sitting almost in shock at the power of those words. Never had I heard someone share so clearly about mystery in the moment of loss, sadness, and what seemed like defeat.

Embracing mystery was a response in complete opposition to what we usually see happen in moments of grief. I know of some who have stopped believing because of loss, or stopped embracing prophecy because a word had not come to pass the way they expected. Refusing to embrace mystery can easily become the birthplace of cessationism; the silencing of prophets; or a journey into unbelief, crippling disappointment, and resentment.

How do we avoid this? We must embrace the apostolic assignment of bringing Heaven to earth, even in the midst of mystery. Mystery and the apostolic go hand in hand. We are unlikely to see everything we believe for this side of eternity, yet the apostolic will never stop pulling Heaven to earth. I believe it will actually find renewed strength to do so as the apostolic ones learn to embrace mystery.

If we believe what Paul says to the Ephesians, that we are seated in Heavenly places, then we have been given a unique starting position. This makes us aware of what is possible, even though we may not get to see it all.

Mystery is also related to childlikeness, which is a characteristic of our faith. Learning to enjoy and embrace mystery is the way of those who are childlike. It leads to questions and will always draw our hearts and minds to a greater reality.

I believe that Bill's message—and the surrounding events—in 2004, was one of the most significant moments of the last twenty years in the story of Bethel and my life. The ability to embrace mystery, to say, "I don't know," even while continuing to pursue the unseen, was, and continues to be, a vital lesson for us all. God is all-knowing and immortal and we are not. There has to be tension between what God knows and what we know. There must also be tension between what we believe to be true and what we get to experience here on earth.

Bill later shared: "If we have no mysteries in our Christian life, then we have reduced our God to our level of understanding." Reducing God in this way would, in effect, make us all gods, and we would end up worshipping our own intelligence and ability, which will always fall short.

Here, then, is the essential understanding of mystery and the apostolic culture. Mystery is an absolute, non-negotiable aspect of the Christian faith.

In our quest to help people, especially after loss, it is tempting to look for answers. But in the midst of looking, sometimes false answers emerge, which are often rooted in pride or deceit. The danger is that we then become deceitful and prideful versus humble, open-minded, and childlike. Pride and deceit are both hazardous states of mind, whereas learning to say "I don't know"—in many different contexts—provides more comfort, honesty, and benefit. "I don't know" is an answer that doesn't settle for a short term fix, it is the launchpad for pursuit and hunger after more of God. The truth is that we really don't know. We don't know why one person was healed and another was not. We don't know why one person gets sick and another does not, and yet we can so easily fall into a dialogue of trying to find an answer.

Mystery may very well be one of the most exciting and fruitful characteristics of an apostolic move of God. In my fifteen years at Bethel, after we learned to embrace mystery, we were privileged to see increase in many areas of life and ministry. This should encourage us all to embrace and steward the mystery in our lives.

Review
How do you handle mystery? Have you been tempted to come up with answers when there aren't any? What could you do, instead?

Declare
What will you declare to reinforce what you have learned today?

Reflect
Reflect on Bill's statement: "I will not ever sacrifice the revelation of God's goodness on an altar of human reasoning to give an answer to a mystery." What stands out to you as you consider it?

"But let him who boasts boast of this, that he understands and knows me, that I am the Lord who exercises lovingkindness, justice, and righteousness on earth; for I delight in these things" declares the Lord.

Jeremiah 9:24

33. Justice

After spending nineteen years in prison management, it should come as no surprise that I have some thoughts on justice; justice as it applies to criminal behavior, as it applies to issues in society and the way in which people groups are treated, but ultimately as it relates to the Kingdom.

The apostolic changes the dynamic of the church. No longer is it merely a sanctuary where people experiencing injustice can run to, but it becomes the place from which reformers are commissioned and sent out. The Christians who make up the Church are sent ones, charged with the assignment to make earth like Heaven. People should therefore be treated according to the culture and principles of Heaven, rather than of earth. That is the subject of justice.

It is important to put a definition on what I call Kingdom justice. Jeremiah 9:24 says that God delights in justice. It is a verse that truly puzzled this ex-prison governor. How can God delight in justice? I have seen so many examples of justice that would not bring delight!

I knew that the verse could not be be based on the earthly model and experience of justice. I concluded that Heaven's justice is based on God being for us, rather than against us—more like the judge of a competition that says we have won than the judge who delivers a punishing judgment. In fact, judgment day in the

Bible will be the day that God judges for those whose names are in the book of life. Yet, we have often presented judgment day as the very opposite.

My resulting definition of Kingdom justice is that its purpose is the restoration of relationships. He will judge for us as those who have chosen to have a relationship with Him. This definition points to, and comes from, the greatest act of justice—and yet the greatest act of injustice—this world has ever witnessed: the crucifixion of Jesus Christ. The outcome of that event is that as we believe in Him, we all have access to be justified, to be made in right standing with God.

As we read the Bible, we see that a principle of justice was established in the garden of Eden. Adam and Eve were removed from the garden not for punishment, but for protection. By removing them, the effect of their sin was not eternal for all of mankind. Instead, it could be pardoned by the power of the blood of Jesus Christ. In other words, they were removed so that one day we could all be invited into the restoration of relationship with God the Father, Son, and Holy Spirit.

Kingdom justice changes our understanding of justice in other realms of life. Let's take criminal behavior, for example. Through the lens of the Kingdom, justice should not start with the punishment of an offender. Rather, the starting point of justice is the goal of creating a safe society in which the majority can live in peace and safety. Decisions of the courts of law should be viewed as a consequence rather than a punishment, the punishment being withdrawal from freedom into a place where they can have the best opportunity of being restored. Of course, not everyone can be or wants to be restored, but that is their responsibility, not ours. Apostolic principles applied to the treatment of offenders must have, at the core, the hope and belief that redemption is for all mankind. With this type of justice, there is no sin so far removed that the person cannot receive forgiveness and begin a journey of redemption, even if they must remain in prison for the rest of their lives.

A Kingdom or apostolic perspective on justice should also change how we view social justice. Social justice is an interesting term which, not so long ago, was not used by Christians and can perhaps be easily misunderstood. I would suggest that, when used by apostolic believers, the term refers to the righting of wrongs done in society that are contrary to the principles of our faith. The wrongs of our society can all be seen through the lens of relational restoration. Often people or groups of people are robbed of relationship and/or the identity of being created in the image of God and worthy of honor. There is a great need for justice as it applies to providing that all mankind be treated with honor and respect as befits those made in the image of God.

Jesus on the cross, in the tomb, His descent into hell, and His resurrection did everything required for all of us to receive justice in this life and the next. Our apostolic assignment is to live out and represent the intention of our Savior. In so doing, we provide everyone with the opportunity to be redeemed and learn how to create safe societies and communities, believing that the treatment of offenders must always carry the heart of redemption, even if that person is never able to be restored to society.

Jesus' act was also for all of mankind, male and female, and every tribe and tongue. Part of our apostolic mandate is correcting mistreatment of any group that is made to feel as though they are not made in the image of God.

Many of us were raised to believe that righteousness was a set of rules and that justice was what happened to us when we broke those rules. The Kingdom truth, however, is that righteousness is an invitation from Heaven to be in right standing with God, and justice is everything we need to accept the invitation. That is the goal for all mankind. But on the way to that goal, we have the great opportunity of modeling the justice of Heaven on earth.

Review
How have you defined justice? How does the author's description of justice here sit with you? Do you find any areas of your heart being challenged? If so, ask God what He wants to tell you.

Declare
What will you declare to reinforce what you have learned today?

Reflect
Reflect on how you see those who offend you. To what extent do you choose to believe the best about them and pursue the restoration of relationship? How can you treat people according to the culture of Heaven, rather than the culture of earth?

From whom the whole body, being fitted and held together by that which every joint supplies, according to the proper working of each individual part, causes the growth of the body for the building up of itself in love.

Ephesians 4:16

34. Excellence

One of my definitions of excellence is when every part serves the whole. Ephesians 4:16 may be the best example of this: the input of the well formed, fitted, and functioning body creating the outcome of growth and being built up in love. And in this case, it is the focus on love which creates excellence.

Another aspect of excellence is that it maximizes what is available in pursuit of the outcome, but it does so in a way that is very different from perfection. Here is a simple comparison between excellence and perfection.

Excellence is sustainable.
We are drawn to it.
It builds the whole.
It points to others, especially the King.
Our heart is drawn to it, it is not about what we do as much as the heart behind what we do.
It knows there is more, yet it is satisfied.

Perfection drives us.
It is not sustainable.
It wears us out.
It points to *us*.
It is results-driven, not input-driven.
There is never enough. It is unsatisfied.

Excellence is actually a very difficult idea to define. Here is an attempt: The internal passions, desires, and sense of purpose that draw us by love, become interwoven into our identity, and are consistently manifested for others to experience and be motivated and inspired by.

If ever there was a word which relates to excellence, it must be love. Love creates the desire for excellence, especially when it is our main focus. That is what we see in Ephesians 4:16. The desire for excellence comes from love; the object is love, and the outcome is everything built up in love. And of course, God is love.

There is no greater motivator than love, a concept Paul describes in this way: "And I show you a still more excellent way" (1 Corinthians 12:31).

The following chapter in the Bible is the most recognized section on love. Yet, we have downgraded 1 Corinthians 13 to merely a nice reading at weddings and special occasions, when, in fact, it is the blueprint for excellence. The picture is clear: whatever we have, if it does not carry love, it is nothing.

I spent over fifteen years in a culture that declared it was a cancer-free zone. That declaration is easily misunderstood, not least because I and others have been diagnosed with cancer while living in that culture. Does that make the statement wrong? That depends on whether you apply a definition of perfection or excellence. If perfection, then the statement fails.

When excellence is applied, the declaration transforms. Excellence is a journey, a desire, and a pursuit. It is the pursuit of an individual or of a company of people whose hearts are drawn, gifts and skills united, and energy pointed in a clear direction.

Excellence and the apostolic are close companions. Both are mindsets to which we are drawn by love and relationships, and both are related to the journey and pursuit of bringing the excellence of Heaven to earth. The success of both will not be measured so much by outcomes as by inputs. Both excellence and the apostolic are conditions of the heart: sent ones drawn by love to take His Excellency wherever we go, whatever we do, and whoever we are.

Review
Read 1 Corinthians 13 again, and consider its list of attributes as they pertain to excellence. What stands out to you?

Declare
What will you declare about excellence in your identity as a sent one?

Reflect
How would you define excellence, compared with perfection? Have you been tempted to pursue perfection? What has that journey been like for you?

If Your presence does not go with us, do not lead us up from here.

Exodus 33:15

35. Worship

It was on a Sunday night when I had perhaps my greatest, but certainly favorite, lesson in worship. Bill Johnson was standing next to me, and as the leader of the meeting, he would send a member of his team up front to close worship when he sensed the right moment. Sunday evenings at Bethel are flexible, and so the decision to close worship is not based on time but on presence and discerning what is happening in the room. As I stood next to Bill after about an hour of worship, he leaned over to me and said, "Watch this." Before I could ask, "Watch what?" he said, "This is her first time leading worship and she has just sung the last song in her set. Don't go up yet, and we will see what she does. This is the test of a great worship leader: what they do when their set list runs out." He then proceeded to whisper to me that she had gone from the outer courts—referencing the old testament tabernacle—into the Holy Place. He saw next that she began to lead us into the Holy of Holies.

That was a lesson I will never forget. It would have been impossible to learn to recognize such a moment outside of that meeting. As minutes went by, the worship leader began to move the congregation back to the Holy Place, and then Bill said to go up front, as it was time. The young worship leader had passed the test; she knew how to take the people beyond the set list and into the Holy of Holies. She is, to this day, one of my favorite worship leaders, and I like nothing more than closing worship when she has been leading. Of course, closing worship is a misnomer and I have recently called it "Maximizing the Moment." Why? Because worship sets everyone up to be aware of the presence of God.

As we view worship throughout history, it gives us varying pictures of how humanity's desire for connection with God's presence has manifested.

Moses clearly understood the need for God's presence as he led the people of Israel. At times, as the Israelites wandered the desert, Moses needed to restore his awareness and refocus his pursuit of God's presence. He understood the importance of worship in making us aware of God's presence, and commissioned the tabernacle as a centerpiece for that worship.

Centuries later, Martin Luther's reforms continued our desire for connecting with God through worship. He introduced the "priesthood of all believers" that led to congregational participation in the singing of hymns, which was previously dominated by priests and choirs that didn't speak or sing in the congregation's native language. This then led to partnerships between preachers and hymn writers—Moody and Sankey, and John and Charles Wesley are just two examples.

From the 1960s, more contemporary praise and worship songs were introduced—along with greater freedom of expression in worship. In the present day, there are some gatherings where the time spent in worship may equal or even exceed the time spent on preaching, because worship sets everyone up to be aware of God's presence. The moves of God of the Jesus People, Vineyard, Toronto, Pensacola, Hillsong, and Bethel have all partnered ministry with music.

This does not mean that previous moves of God, those not focused on worship, did not value the presence of God, but to fail to acknowledge what is happening today would be equally incorrect. So what is different?

Heaven came to earth in the form of Jesus: Immanuel, God with us. And now we, the sent ones, have Him with us as we are filled the the Spirit, and have Christ in us, the hope of glory. Continually experiencing the presence of God in corporate meetings trains us to know that He is with us in every circumstance of life.

Songs and hymns carry words we are more likely to remember than the preaching, but this season is much more than just partnering songs with preaching. It is about His presence. We have always been called to "go," but this apostolic sending culture is teaching us to see that not only have we been sent, but as we go, we need to say, "God, if [Your] presence does not go with us, don't send us." The apostolic desire to bring Heaven to earth requires us to know the experience of His presence in every scenario, circumstance, and emotion of life.

Being trained as I was that Sunday night is something we can all experience in different ways. As we train our senses, we will know His presence, prompting, and guiding when we are reading His word, enjoying His creation, spending time with others, or even in the midst of great trials and challenges.

We are, quite simply, being trained in the presence for the assignment of bringing Heaven to earth and expanding the influence of King Jesus wherever we go, whatever we do, and whoever we are.

Review
How have you seen moves of God and worship go together? How has God used worship in your own walk with Him?

Declare
What will you declare to reinforce what you have learned today?

Reflect
Write (or listen to) a song that captures the current expression of God you are seeing in your own life or ministry. What is God saying to you as you write/sing/listen?

Now faith is the assurance of things hoped for, the conviction of things not seen.

Hebrews 11:1

36. Faith and Hope

Faith, by its very nature, is connected to the unseen. The struggle of faith is that we often lose sight of its nature and review our faith in light of our circumstances and the result—or lack of result—of our prayers.

Faith has eyes that can see what we cannot. Repentance changes the way we think, but faith changes the way we see. My friend Leif Hetland talks of seeing with Heaven's eyes. These are the apostolic eyes, seeing from the perspective of Heaven.

As soon as we reduce our faith to the natural, the material, or the evidence we see, we are in danger. The apostolic starts in the unseen of Heaven and brings that to earth. An apostolic move of God may include practical and physical structures, organizations, and results, but it cannot be reduced to only that. When we remove the unseen of Heaven, the result is form without power, a result we're familiar with in the history of the church.

The apostolic has faith at its heart.

Faith is unscientific, yet its fruit is measured scientifically, even when it defies science. Faith is not dependent on mathematics or formulas—the amount of faith is not related to outcome. Jesus honors little faith and great faith.

Faith is above psychology and emotions, but its outcome affects every part of our being. It is illogical, yet the wisdom received by faith confounds the minds of the greatest philosophers and thinkers. Faith does not bow to the rules of earth, but acts in, through, and with them.

Faith is transcendent yet incarnate, but through Jesus can be in us all. It is impossible to understand, yet impossible to live without. Faith is rooted in the identity of the I Am who revealed Himself to Moses, and the I Am that is Jesus who revealed Himself to us all. Faith is now but not yet, seen yet unseen, proven yet requires untested steps. No dictionary can define it, no rules can limit it, no argument can rob us of it, no scheme can transcend it, no obstacle can stop it. Faith IS.

Faith is the primary core of our Christianity. It must influence the preaching of the gospel by the evangelist and we must ensure that our teaching and pastoring is not relegated to what we see and experience, rather than what we believe and have hope for.

The revelation that the apostolic and prophetic are the foundation of the Church is directly related to faith. The apostle and prophet operate in the unseen, their gifts are made evident by faith. The Apostle Paul wrote twice in his letter to the Romans about the obedience of faith. This sums up the tension, but with it, the necessity that the unseen work of faith must always be included.

Faith and the apostolic. It is an obvious partnership. As is faith and hope.

In Romans 5:5, the Apostle Paul states that, "Hope does not disappoint." I have often pondered this apparently outrageous verse. I can easily find myself questioning it on the basis that I and others have not always seen the outcome we hoped for.

So how can it be said that hope does not disappoint?

In Proverbs 13:12, we read that "Hope deferred makes the heart sick, but desire fulfilled is a tree of life."

Are these two verses contradicting? One appears to say that hope doesn't disappoint, while the other says that when we don't get what we hoped for, it makes us sick.

But what if we're misinterpreting the verse in Proverbs? It is not that we don't get what we hoped for, which makes us sick, it is that we stop hoping. When we stop hoping, we create an alternative appointment for our destiny.

Hope is a way of life, and I suggest an apostolic one, modeled by Paul very clearly. Hope is a mindset that creates a culture, which causes us to see things through the lens of Heaven, where the God of all hope is ever present (Romans 15:13).

As I mentioned previously, Paul wrote his letter to the Romans after he had written to the Corinthians, giving a list of the tests and trials of his life and ministry. Few, I suspect, have endured so much for the sake of the gospel—an outcome that Jesus prophesied at Paul's moment of conversion.

It is in the context of tribulations and tough seasons that Paul wrote Romans 5. He said that as we exult in our tribulations, we grow in endurance and character and that this produces hope, a hope that does not disappoint.

When we start to realize that, as sent ones, we are part of something bigger than ourselves, we see that hope appoints us as ambassadors—as more than conquerors in the great story of Heaven. We become ambassadors of hope. We carry a message that Paul articulated in Romans 8:28 and 38-39. I paraphrase Romans 8:28 as, "He wastes nothing, He gets me ready."

Hope in the context of the New Testament, as we know well from Hebrews, is related to faith. Faith is the evidence of things hoped for. Hope, therefore, fuels our faith. We are not fueled by experience or outcome, but by Heaven and its Royal Family who made us, saved us, sent us, live in us, and empower us.

When we live from Heaven to earth, we are sent on an assignment. Hope appoints us to the correct assignment. Heaven-originated hope cannot disappoint because it will never send us to the wrong assignment or appointment. The strategies of our enemy and the fallen nature of earth and its inhabitants may cause things to go against us. But as we enter the presence of God and exult in our tribulations, even these things will produce perseverance, character, and hope.

Hope is therefore a posture, a mindset. It is how we position ourselves and how we see, so we do not need to be dependent on outcomes. Once we realize this, we better understand the essence of what Paul was saying—hope does not disappoint. Rather, it appoints us. Seeing from Heaven's perspective and expecting the heart of Heaven to be displayed allows us to pursue life in a manner that inspires and energizes us. The medical and scientific world affirms this, containing much evidence that hope is good for us.

When I think of the alternative, which is to see everything through the lens of hopelessness, I know what I will choose.

Hope is a sketch on a canvas that invites the master painter to complete the painting. Even if it is not completed according to our imagination or expectation, it is still a work of art designed for good.

Faith and biblical hope are inseparable. When we hope without faith, the object of our faith becomes luck. Faith without hope, on the other hand, lacks the focus and purpose which hope brings.

Review
Do you see primarily through a lens of hope or of hopelessness? To what extent have you allowed disappointment to tint your lens? Read Romans 5:5 and Proverbs 13:12. What is highlighted to you as you ponder these verses?

Declare
What will you declare to place your focus on hope and faith this week?

Reflect
What assignment have you been appointed to? Reflect on the promises God has given you to hope for in that assignment.

For God so loved the world

That He sent His only son.

John 3:16

37. Sonship and Inner Healing

It would be almost impossible to read this far and not see the connection between the apostolic and sonship. Sonship is, in many respects, the starting place for the apostolic. Jesus is the sent Son, the sent one, sent by His Father into the world to save the world. He is the role model for being sent and the role model for sonship. Not only that, but His purpose is that we are restored to sonship and daughtership with our Heavenly father.

But sonship doesn't stop at being sent. Sonship affects every aspect of our lives as Christians. Perhaps one of the most remarkable aspects of the life of Jesus is that, although He was the Son who was sent, He came as a baby, grew up as a child, and experienced the public affirmation of being called the Son of God (adoption) at His baptism. This sequence is the evidence of Isaiah 9:6: "A child is born, a son is given."

These events were then followed by His public ministry and the demonstration of His authority as the sent Son of God. Through Jesus' public ministry, we see that the government is on the shoulders of this Son, demonstrated through extraordinary authority over sickness, demons, storms, death, and lack.

Physically, the picture of something being on our shoulders illustrates submission to the head and connection to every part of the body. This picture represents two things: a non-negotiable connection to the head (the Father), and complete integration and alignment with the whole body.

As we read on in scripture, we see that one of the titles of this Son is Prince of Peace. A prince is surely the ultimate description of a son: one who knows who they are, who their identity comes from, what their purpose is, and where they are going. A prince is secure, as was the Son of God.

We must demonstrate the character of sons if we are to represent the Father and the Son. It is that which will enable us to be sent in the manner and with the authority of Heaven's government. And that is where the third member of the Trinity steps fully into our lives, releasing the Spirit of Adoption.

These past few decades, we have seen a rise in awareness, teaching, books, conferences, and ministries focused on restoring our relationships as sons and daughters of God, while also bringing healing to our relational dysfunctions on earth. An inner healing movement and an apostolic move of God are happening at the same time, not out of coincidence, but because they are essential to each other and actually need each other.

When we focus on sending people out to expand the influence of the Kingdom, our need to be secure in our identity (both as leaders and those who are sent) increases. In fact, when we do not teach and embrace our identity as healthy sons and daughters, an empowering apostolic move of God is in danger of reverting to a hierarchical, competitive, and controlling model.

The vast majority of inner healing is ultimately connected to relational issues. In other words, inner healing directly touches on our identities as sons and daughters, fathers and mothers, and secure men and women who are able to lead out of identity rather than dysfunction.

An apostolic move of God is about sending people into the world and trusting people to know who they are and to behave accordingly. Insecure people will easily revert to fear and control and will fail to give people the opportunity to find their full potential. When we allow inner healing to restore our identity and security, we will raise what I call "big people," and send them into places we have no access and no control. This is the point of trust: when we allow them to express themselves in those environments from a place of secure knowledge of their sonship.

Empowered sent ones must know who they are. The potential for failing in our empowered assignment means that our identity must be in who we are, rather than what we achieve or fail to achieve. The insecure person with an orphan heart is more liable to find their identity in successful performance or in the shame of failure. The son or daughter, on the other hand, is more likely to find purpose and security in their identity as a child of the King.

My relational wounds need to be healed up so that I am able to relate to my Heavenly Father and to those around me. The response of an orphan heart will lead to performance, control, a "poor me" attitude, a "never enough" way of thinking, and a jealous and competitive approach to anyone demonstrating strength or success. A good way of summing up the orphan heart is that it is fundamentally trapped in a mindset of deficiency and lack. It will, therefore, be drawn to manipulating and controlling people and circumstances in order to replace lack with counterfeit comfort.

The apostolic is the mindset of increase. It partners with dreaming, risking, trusting, hoping, and believing. Isaiah prophesies that there would be *no end to the increase* of the government built on the shoulders of a son.

You cannot have a lasting apostolic move of God without a corresponding increase in inner healing, the experience of sonship, and the experience of the Father heart of God. Not only does each need the other, they are also, in many respects, the same thing expressed differently. The apostolic is about being sent by the Father. Inner healing restores our identity as sons. Sonship ensures that we are able to receive and engage with everything the Father has for us, and therefore that we will carry with us all that is available.

Without sonship, we will not:

Carry Heaven's full and available authority
Govern in security of identity and purpose
Pass the baton to the next generation

For those who have spent time reading books on the Father heart of God, received counseling and ministry to heal relational wounds, attended Father Heart conferences, or ministered to others in these ways, thank you! You are a vital part of creating an apostolic culture. You may have thought that you did it because that was your need, your gift, your experience, and that you wanted to see people set free as sons and daughters. But the gift of sonship, which is the result of pursuing the Father's heart, will affect the whole earth as we see this apostolic move of God fulfill Heaven's mandate. It is a gift for a generation and a movement.

As I mentioned previously, I love the parable of the prodigal son. As I teach it, I like to dream of how that house must have looked after the young son returned and the elder brother realized the father has always been with him. I like to call it post-prodigal. This, I believe, is the invitation of the apostolic: living from a place of knowing that we are considered worthy, trusted sons and daughters, who are celebrated at home and sent out with the father's presence and provision going with us. Sons and daughters do not need to leave to find their identity, they find it at home and are then sent out to reproduce their home wherever they go.

Review
How secure would you say you are in your identity? How have you embraced the healing of past wounds so you are free and secure enough to empower others?

Declare
What will you declare to reinforce what you have learned today?

Reflect
Reflect on your own journey of sonship. To what extent have you embraced the spirit of adoption? How has this influenced you in your life and ministry?

I Paul, send you Timothy,

to remind them of my works in Christ.

1 Corinthians 4:17 (my paraphrase)

38. Covering

It is fairly common in some church circles to talk of covering or being covered. I myself have, on a number of occasions, spoken about or referenced the subject of spiritual covering, while always being aware that this can be a contentious subject.

The word "covering" is not directly the language of the Bible. Yet, we do see that Paul sent Timothy, which could be interpreted as a kind of covering. This was not a controlling covering, but instead it was the apostolic covering of a loving, proud dad, confident in the exploits of his son and knowing that the son will represent the father. If we understand the empowering nature of the apostolic, then we can begin to see that covering, when provided from an apostolic viewpoint, will itself empower instead of control.

Think of an umbrella. I meet many people who have experienced covering in the form of someone holding an umbrella over their head. I am sure that I am not alone in finding that when someone else holds the umbrella, I run the risk of being poked in the eye, my head getting scratched, or getting rained on. This is akin to a covering extended in a form of a more controlling approach. We can have our vision impaired, our heads hurt, and we still get rained on.

The covering that I prefer is when I am given an umbrella and I choose whether or not to raise it. As I walk, I am able to adjust it without impairing my vision or having my head—in other words, my thoughts and dreams—affected. Even if the rain should be blowing in my face in a gale, I can move the covering in front of me. It is also more of a multi-colored covering because we can find and choose a variety of coverings from a variety of people. After all, Paul told the Corinthians that they had many teachers and yet not many fathers, which implies that we are able to have many fathers.

When we consider how Paul sent Timothy, it is very clear that Paul was commissioned to do the works of Christ and that Timothy was sent to remind others of Paul's works in Christ. True sons are able to position themselves to receive from fathers because they can, through the maturity of sonship, choose those attributes which remind them of Jesus and overlook those that don't.

I do not desire to travel or minister on life's journey alone. Yes, my covering is Christ, but it is also found in the commission of those who I choose to consider fathers, some of whom I have not met.

It is understandable that if the covering we experienced in our past involved control, or caused hurt, we may be tempted to reject covering and defend our rejection of it by pointing to the absence of the concept in the Bible.

The problem is not in covering itself, but that covering imposed without relationship is more likely to carry elements of control.

Too often we have seen covering in the context of an organization and structure, which creates rules and agreement over points of doctrine and develops systems to ensure compliance. Although all of those have their place, if they are motivated by control and are the first way of looking at people, they will reap the consequences of unresolved conflicts, misunderstanding, and broken relationships.

Instead, I prefer to see covering as allowing myself to be commissioned to carry out the vision of a father or mother. Then I can position myself to be covered by a leader who represents Christ. Even when I may have no direct relationship with them, I can benefit from their life and experience having gone ahead of me. If I have the heart posture of a son or daughter, I will receive from them as I position myself to honor their lives and teachings. So I try to live with my heart available to receive Heaven through one of Heaven's representatives. I am free to choose and to reposition my heart if Christ is not represented by them in some areas, but that does not give me license to criticize or to stop loving them.

Those who have been hurt by abusive covering can find great freedom in receiving their umbrella and choosing the segments of that umbrella they wish to use—the messages and commissioning of many fathers to do the work of Christ. Of course, as in the natural, we will have primary fathers, but we will also find the "in-laws through marriage" as we connect with a variety of families across the earth. Covering is not about control, but protection, favor, and support. It is an image of the things we receive through our covering from Christ. Covering will always be connected to the positioning of our hearts, and it always results in empowerment.

A covering enables us to go with the grace of someone else's anointing and experience, with the awareness that someone is covering us in prayer, and with a heart that is able to receive. That is the way of the Kingdom and the apostolic.

Review
How does your perspective of covering change as you read the author's description here? Is this a kind of covering that you could embrace?

What can you do to provide father-focused, apostolic covering for those you lead or influence? What would it look like to do that well?

Declare
What will you declare to reinforce what you have learned today?

Reflect
Reflect on your experience of covering. Is there anyone you need to forgive? What is God saying about this area?

For I know the plans I have for you,

says the Lord.

Jeremiah 29:11

39. Destiny

I don't really like the word destiny. As I was growing up, destiny was not a word used very much in my Christian circles. For me, and many others, it belonged outside of the church and contained within it a sense of fate rather than a choice made in relationship with a loving Father. In fact, it is not really a biblical word unless you include the cup of fate that the Jews drank in Babylon, as referenced in Isaiah 65:11.

That shift from a fate-filled understanding of destiny to something that stems from relationship with a good Father is related to the apostolic. Being sent as sons and daughters is central to an apostolic movement, but being sent is not an autocratic act—it comes from relationship.

There are a number of shifts in our mindset and approach to the idea of destiny that I have observed in recent years:

> *From fate and no control, to participation and co-laboring*
> *From the sense that a painful destiny is confirmation of willingness to pay a price, to discovering passion*
> *From slaves, to sons and daughters*
> *From doing and delivering first, to discovering what God has hidden for you*

The apostolic represents a family approach to life. Being sent from a family to represent and reproduce the family requires a sense of connection and joy in being sent. Sending is also a condition of the heart rather than an act of autocratic leadership. As an apostolic people who represent Jesus, the first apostle, we need look no further than Him to gain an understanding of apostolic destiny.

> *Jesus knew who He was (I am the way, the truth and the life, I am the good shepherd, etc.)*
> *Jesus knew why He was here (I came to serve not to be served)*
> *Jesus knew where He was going (I go to prepare a place for you)*
> *Jesus knew the impact of His life (Whoever believes in Me shall not perish but have everlasting life)*

This list mirrors how I define big people. The relationship between these two is clear. Big people have a destiny, and people who know their destiny become those who bring change and transformation.

The desire for destiny in our world is rightly important, although it may be true that it is more of a first world desire. Five hundred years ago, the concept of destiny was less of a challenge; all that was required, then, was to look at our birth certificate and follow our dads to work. If we read that our name was Smith, then we knew that the blacksmith's shop would be in our future.

Perhaps, in that simplicity, is a clue to navigating the modern day complexities and choices we face. We check our identity and follow our Heavenly Dad to work.

I love destiny discovery, but I know that there is no single formula. For so many of us, discovering our destiny is a journey. Some may have a very clear sense of a call to do or to go, while others may pursue ability development, and still others follow what is beautiful to them. What I have discovered is what I call the beauty of the dance. The psalmist says: "Our steps are ordered by the Lord" (Psalm 37:23). I expect many, like me, interpreted this verse to describe a regimented path of ordered steps, but I have begun to see that sometimes these ordered steps are a dance. The essential element is that our steps are in step with His.

For those on the path of uncovering your destiny, here are a few simple keys I've found useful in our approach to destiny discovery:

> *What do you love? Knowing that He created us to see and experience things, discovering what we love invites Him to give us those desires.*
> *What are you afraid of? Our fears can be clues too. So often, what we have been made afraid of is the opposite of something we can or should do.*
> *What are your testimonies? Our testimonies are incredibly powerful as there is an inherent component of our victories which wants to see them happen again.*
> *What is He telling you? And of course, our prophetic words and dreams help us identify the Lord's leading.*

My greatest encouragement to us all, however, is to believe that He wastes nothing and He gets us ready. It is my paraphrase of

Romans 8:28. As we believe and trust our stories with God, we find confidence and authority to step out on the foundation of what God has done already.

Our destinies are so entwined with Heaven that they are apostolic, and we must bring them from our seat in the Heavenly places, with the power of the testimony, prophetic encounters, and dreams.

Review
Go through the things Jesus knew about Himself (who He was, why He was here, etc). How would you describe yourself under each of these headings? Ask God what He wants to tell you.

Declare
What will you declare about your destiny as a sent one?

Reflect
Reflect on the author's list of keys for uncovering destiny. How would you answer each of the four questions?

We were like those who dreamed.

Psalm 126:1

40. Dreams

We are sent from Heaven to earth to make earth like Heaven. That is the apostolic and our role within it. As we live out our apostolic purpose, we must remember that every attribute of Heaven has an earthly counterpart. But, in order to see Heaven on earth, we need to be able to dream.

I believe that man was created to dream: to desire, to aspire to something greater than where they currently find themselves. Children so easily dream and imagine—their limitless expectation of life and their own potential is the beauty of childhood and a characteristic of childlikeness. If dreaming is absent, however, then a culture, society, or family is limited to what *is*, accepting what life throws at them, limited by what is seen and what has already been done.

In Psalm 126, we see that the captive ones of Zion dreamed while in captivity, so we learn that captivity does not limit dreaming. When the people were released, they were able to say, "We were like those who dreamed." But in order to stand in the future and pinch ourselves, wondering if we are still dreaming, we have to dream in the first place.

The nature and context of our dreams can be interpreted through the parable of the sower and the seed. If the dream is the seed, it can fall onto various types of ground. Dreams need the correct environment in which to grow or come to pass. That soil is not the culture that surrounds us, but the culture within us and within those with whom we do life. All of the types of soil in the parable apply to dreams. Will they fall on the pathway, amongst the shallow soil, be choked by weeds, or find the fertile soil in which to grow?

Dreams not only need the right soil to grow, but also a culture of permission to dream in the first place. We lose our capacity to dream when our vision is limited to what we can see or what we have seen in the past. We also lose our capacity to dream when our culture stifles dreams. That is where the apostolic comes in.

Combining the nature of our role as sent ones from Heaven to earth, and the assignment contained in the prayer Jesus taught of everything in Heaven being on earth, we should view every aspect of life on earth as a potential container for Heaven. In other words, we should look at life on earth and dream of it revealing and replicating Heaven.

The famous sermon by Peter on the day of Pentecost includes the phrase that "young men will dream dreams." It is a part of the baptism of the Holy Spirit that we should dream and see visions. The whole Trinity is involved: the Son has sent us, the Father gives us desires, and the Holy Spirit empowers us to dream.

In the natural, our planet has been transformed by men and women who saw in their minds what couldn't be seen with their eyes. People who looked at birds that fly and said, why not us? Impossible scenarios were envisioned in dreams long before they were seen. Men and women have done extraordinary things, with and without a relationship with God, and allowed their minds and imaginations to create a constantly evolving world.

I believe that it is time for men and women who are made in the image of God, filled with the Spirit, have Christ in them—the hope of glory—and are part of a company that has the mind of Christ, to dream with God for the benefit of mankind and themselves.

It's time for apostolic dreamers who are no longer limited by the restrictions of what is already possible. It is time for dreams to pull Heaven to earth and dream, pursue, and imagine the world that was in the heart of God when He created it.

Our world is full of extraordinary people who have achieved amazing developments. The truth is that many have not known God. They have used their God-given, made-in-His-image ability to achieve these things. In a way, they have filled the earth with the knowledge of their glory. Yes, there is a glory from being made in the image of God, even without knowing Him.

The apostolic culture removes from us some of the restrictions that may have held us back in the past. Religious control, false expectations of careers which Christians should pursue, and not allowing the creative dreamers to dream have kept many believers from being the world changers that we now see bringing global change without a relationship with the Creator.

Now is our time: to dream, to take our place, to bring the change the world needs, and use it to bring glory to God.

Review
How have dreams played a part in your life? In what ways do your dreams need an upgrade?

Declare
What will you declare to reinforce what you have learned today?

Reflect
Reflect on your ability to dream. Has captivity or disappointment affected you? Take it to God. What does He want to tell you about it?

He called His disciples to Him;

and chose twelve of them,

Whom He also named as apostles.

Luke 6:13

41. Discipleship

It may seem strange to leave discipleship until the end of this book. In reality, the whole book is a discipleship workbook, but not, perhaps, the model of discipleship we usually think of.

Jesus called the twelve to be disciples and titled them as apostles before His death. This has often caught my eye. It appears in both Matthew 10:2 and Luke 6:13.

There is no doubt that discipleship and the apostolic must go together. As we see the church become truly apostolic, we must also disciple believers to be apostolic.

Salvation and preaching the gospel must be followed by discipleship. Yet, that discipleship must not only lead to sharing the gospel, but to fulfilling the assignment of being sent from Heaven to earth and expanding the influence of King Jesus.

If we are to move beyond pastoring and church as the primary goal, and see the apostolic and advancement of the Kingdom as central to our assignment, then we need to expand our curriculum of discipleship.

Jesus called the disciples but saw them as apostles very early in His ministry. This is apostolic discipleship: seeing beyond the newly saved Christian to a mature man or woman representing Christ in every sphere of influence on earth.

I have been in environments where someone with a successful career became a Christian and immediately experienced pressure to enter into career ministry. That may, at times, be an appropriate goal, but it is often the result of a church-focused culture rather than an apostolic one. A good friend of mine admitted to me that in twenty-five years of church ministry, that was always his view: getting successful and talented people saved, discipled, and eventually into career ministry and ordination.

I had the opposite life experience. For twenty-five years, I served in hospitals and prisons, knowing I was called into career ministry. As soon as I arrived in the church setting, I adopted the job description of sending people out of church-focused ministry and into Kingdom-centered ministry wherever they found themselves.

I am not sure that we have seen this approach developed as much as is needed. Schools of ministry, which are becoming more common, equip believers for an apostolic assignment, especially reinforcing the truth that every believer is a supernatural minister. That is a great start, but there is more.

Apostolic discipleship embraces the supernatural and equips the saints as supernatural ministers in every area of life, but it also goes beyond that. Apostolic discipleship raises sons and daughters, provides destiny discovery, erases the secular-sacred divide, and creates an apostolic family of those who serve both inside and outside of the church.

The example of Jesus must be ours: seeing the new follower as a future apostolic sent one. Revival, societal transformation, and a new renaissance glorifying God depend on it.

Review
How have you defined discipleship in the past? What aspects of apostolic discipleship challenge your previous way of thinking?

Declare
What will you declare about apostolic discipleship either for yourself or others?

Reflect
Reflect on times you've felt equipped, empowered, and sent outside of the church setting. How can you create that same environment for others within your sphere of influence?

As the Father sent me,

so I send you.

John 20:21

42. Sent

It was on the first day of the week, when Jesus rose from the grave, that He appeared to the disciples. I assume there were ten present at the time. Thomas was absent, as was Judas.

What a day that was for those ten who had walked with Jesus for three years and had been with Him in everything. At the end of a chaotic and dramatic weekend, they must have been afraid that their way of life had come to an abrupt end. Perhaps they were processing the painful experience of one of their own betraying Jesus and sending Him to the cross.

And of course, they must have felt powerless. They were used to seeing the demonstration of power in circumstances of death, disease, lack, and demonic possession. Yet, on that first resurrection Sunday, I imagine they were confused, scared, struggling with emotions regarding a friend, and powerless.

It was into this that Jesus appeared with the answers to every need and concern. He offered the disciples peace, power (through the Holy Spirit), a lesson on the importance of forgiveness (certainly addressing their hearts toward Judas), and then He offered them purpose. "As the Father sent me, so I send you."

With a sense of the conclusion of His earthly assignment, He launched all who believe and will believe too continue the assignment.

As I write and teach about the importance of being apostolic and knowing that we are sent I cannot fail to see the parallels to that evening of the first resurrection Sunday.

Our world is chaotic, full of strife and confusion, a world which needs the peace that passes all understanding and the representatives of the Prince of Peace to declare that His peace transcends all circumstances.

So many situations can leave us feeling powerless when we use earth's resources alone. We need to receive the Holy Spirit, and with that power, continue the movement Jesus initiated.

Conflict both in and out of the church has become an overwhelming part of our lives. Criticisms, judgements, and negative behaviors create a toxic environment for our hearts. We must learn again to forgive; the responsibility continues to be ours. The Judas 'spirit' is alive and well, yet we cannot blame others or wait for their wake up and repentance, it is for us to forgive for our own benefit first.

And so He sends us. It began then and continues now. A Heavenly assignment into a world with no lesser need than those ten disciples had that evening.

We need the apostolic, carrying forgiveness, peace, and power. It is available, and it is our assignment.

As we have seen throughout history and even in our present church culture, the apostolic is at times associated with hierarchy and control.

A structure that controls and exercises power eventually becomes a structure that tells people where they must go. If that model were based on Heaven, it would suggest that when Jesus was sent from Heaven to earth, He was forced against His will. I prefer to believe that the decision was a result of a family discussion, and that being sent was an inside job as far as Jesus was concerned.

So, too, is the act of being sent for all of us. As we embrace the Father's vision for our lives, we enter into a divine covenant. Not one that goes against our will, but a marriage of two wills inextricably linked and living for the benefit of each other and the fruit of their relationship.

I often reflect on the story told in Luke 15, usually referred to as the parable of the prodigal son. I prefer to call it the parable of the extravagantly loving father. In the story, the younger brother went (instead of being sent), and as a result, had to return home when he had no other options. His return was greeted with outrageous, undeserved and extravagant love.

After experiencing his father's embrace, if he were to continue that level of connection with his father, then should that boy ever leave home again, I would expect him to be sent. He would experience a mutual sending: a father who trusts him to know who he is, and a son with the character to represent the father—all because he discovered, through extravagance, how much he is loved and believed in.

Being sent is an act of representing and reproducing. One illustration of this is the daughter who is given in marriage. To be given in marriage by a father has nothing to do with the giving away of property: it is an act of great love and trust. The father giving a daughter is saying to her and her husband, "I trust you to go and represent and reproduce your family with this man." It is an act of handing over primary relationship, an act of covenant.

As we are sent in an apostolic culture, that sending comes with an inside awareness that our going is blessed by those with whom we have relationship, and it is validated by the principles of those who father/mother and influence us. Let me explain this a little more. If the teaching and exhortation at church on a Sunday affirms that I am sent (apostolic) and that my day job is not a second class ministry, then that changes my approach to the rest of my week. When I am in my office, classroom, or at home, I carry an inner awareness that I am sent, valued, seen, and known for my contribution. It does not matter that I work or serve outside of the more traditional ministry expressions.

To be sent is an act of interdependence, a mutually beneficial and honoring relationship. Destiny, discovery, and purpose in life shifts when we embrace a loving, good Father. Being sent is not about being told what to do, but rather a co-laboring and co-discovering experience.

When my Heavenly Father directs me, that direction is not built on control, but on love, trust, and honor. If I believe that God is love, that He has my best interests at heart while writing me into His beautiful plans for eternity, then there is no reason for me not to bring my life into submission to a perfectly good God.

Consequently, as we reveal the Father, our leadership as sent ones causes us to lead from that same position of love. We will send and be sent out of divine purpose and the fulfillment of our destiny, in relationship with our Heavenly Father.

Review
Read Luke 15. What elements of the apostolic do you see in the younger brother, the older brother, the servants, and the father in this parable from Jesus?

Declare
What will you declare to remind yourself that you are sent?

Reflect
Reflect on how you've previously viewed "being sent." Has it been controlling or life-giving for you? What manner of sending have you cultivated in your own life or ministry?

Conclusion: An Apostolic Commission

I commission you, reader, no matter your position or career. You are an apostolic glory carrying leader, mother, pastor, person, CEO, doctor, teacher, or worker, bringing Heaven to earth and establishing and expanding the Kingdom. This is no small task, but God has called, chosen, and gifted you for such a time as this.

Isaiah 61 serves as our reminder and encouragement that this is our call. It begins with the Spirit of God on a man, declaring that the broken-hearted be bound up. Perhaps that was you, broken-hearted because you didn't feel valuable or didn't know where you belonged. Or maybe you felt more like the prisoner or captive. Whichever it is, the declaration is the same, "The Spirit of the Lord God is upon me, because the Lord has anointed me to bring good news to the afflicted; He has sent me to bind up the broken-hearted, to proclaim liberty to captives and freedom to prisoners; to proclaim the favorable year of the Lord and the day of vengeance of our God; to comfort all who mourn" (Isaiah 61:1-2). You are free and healed up and you can watch the great exchanges of oil for mourning, beauty for ashes, and all things reversed in your life.

Further into the chapter in Isaiah 61, we are reminded that it is not the anointed one who rebuilds, restores, and raises up, but those set free who perform these great transformational tasks.

That is you. You are set free to bring transformation, to bring Heaven to earth. From there, Isaiah shows us the outcome: prosperity and wealth with new identities of priests and ministers. And finally, instead of shame, a double portion (Isaiah 61:3-7).

This is the promise I have for you. And as I write and commission you, I pray and declare you are free to be who God made you to be, free to carry your gift with healthy pride, free to rebuild, restore, and raise up. You are a sent one and the next reformation, revival, or renaissance needs you to complete the great promise of the priesthood of all believers and work fearlessly toward a united bride, "That they may be one, just as We are one" (John 17:22).

And so I pray and declare that you will:

> See the greater works that Jesus prophesied (John 14:12).
>
> Experience the greater revelation that Isaiah prophesied (Isaiah 64:4; 1 Cor 2:9).
>
> Enjoy the increase of government on the shoulders of a Son (Isaiah 9:6-7).
>
> Grow from glory to glory as you see Christ in others (2 Cor 3:18).

And in all things, know your apostolic assignment as a sent one, whoever you are, wherever you go, and whatever you do (John 17:8).

In the name of Jesus, in the power of the Holy Spirit, and to God be the glory.

Amen!

If you have enjoyed this book then you will enjoy and benefit from:

Your Divine Purpose Community

Monthly 90 minute on-line school night
(every 3 months an extended combined 2 hour school)

Includes WHITEBOARD COACHING Demonstration

Monday Themes

1-3   Believing Your Story: Releasing confidence & authority.
4-6   Your Manifesto: What happens when you fully show up.
7-9   Encounters: Maximising their benefit to you & others.
10-12 Maintaining Your Momentum: Keys for staying strong.

Wednesday Themes

1-3   Taking Your Place: Revival-Reformation-Renaissance
4-6   Living apostolically: Knowing you are SENT.
7-9   Creating Increase: Culture & Strategy.
10-12 Leading Teams & Leaders. Inspiring others.

Monthly coaching newsletter

Access to pre recorded resources including:
Strategic Planning-Mastering Kingdom Administration
Apostolic Masterclass - Empowering Leadership
Things Fathers Do - You are Sent

Join NOW
paulmanwaring.com

For other resources go to paulmanwaring.com

Paul has a number of resources available & is constantly developing new ones.

Some of the primary themes are:

Strategic Planning
Personal & Organisational Coaching
Creating an Apostolic Family
Mastering Kingdom Administration

Other Books:
What on Earth is Glory
Kisses from a Good God
Things Fathers Do
(Available on Amazon, & shop.bethel.com)

You can also follow Paul at:

Instagram	paul_manwaring
Facebook:	Paul Manwaring
Twitter:	Paul_Manwaring
YouTube:	PaulSueM

The definition you place on Glory will determine where you expect to encounter it!

Surgery is not a second-class healing.

Fatherhood: The opportunity it presents us, both as fathers & mothers, is that of revealing to the world the greatest father of all: our Father in heaven.

Printed in Great Britain
by Amazon